J'ACCUSE…!

(POEM *VERSUS* SILENCE)

J'Accuse...!

(POEM *VERSUS* SILENCE)

GEORGE ELLIOTT CLARKE

EXILE
editions

singular fiction, poetry, nonfiction, translation, drama, and graphic books

Library and Archives Canada Cataloguing in Publication

Title: J'accuse...! : (poem versus silence) / George Elliott Clarke.
  Names: Clarke, George Elliott, author.
Identifiers: Canadiana (print) 20210292091 | Canadiana (ebook) 20210292105 |
  ISBN 9781550969535 (softcover) | ISBN 9781550969542 (EPUB) |
  ISBN 9781550969559 (Kindle) | ISBN 9781550969566 (PDF)
Classification: LCC PS8555.L3748 J33 2021 | DDC C811/.54—dc23

J'Accuse…! (Poem Versus *Silence)* is a work that versifies animadversion – glossed by imagination. Yet, the persons discussed and the events chronicled are not imaginary, but attested to by publicly available documents. (Still, poetic license colours some descriptions.) Authorial judgement of identified individuals arises solely from what those actors have said or written or done, and all's borne witness to by court testimony or press comment or personal correspondence or telephone communication. Some anonymous persons – and/or generic "estates" – win rebuke for illiberal behaviour, or for intolerant sentiments. They know who they are.

Note: The author deviates occasionally from Standard English orthography. Presume a deliberate accent on "difference" rather than the accidental deviance of a "typo."

We gratefully acknowledge the Government of Canada and Ontario Creates for their support toward our publishing activities.

All Exile Editions books are published independantly of financial assistance from the Canada Council for the Arts's or the Ontario Arts Council's Book Publishing: Block Grant programs.

Canadian sales representation: The Canadian Manda Group,
664 Annette Street, Toronto ON M6S 2C8.
www.mandagroup.com 416 516 0911.

North American and international distribution, and U.S. sales:
Independent Publishers Group, 814 North Franklin Street,
Chicago IL 60610 www.ipgbook.com toll free: 1 800 888 4741.

your shiver is an outpouring of Beauty.
—RAED ANIS AL-JISHI, "The Woodenness of a Letter"

I terrify ugliness,
with independent Beauty.
—BÄNOO ZAN, "Iran"

Denn das Schöne *ist nichts*
als des Schrecklichen Anfang…
—RAINER MARIA RILKE, "Die Erste Elegie"

À

Anna Mae Aquash (1945-1975)

&

Helen Betty Osborne (1952-1971)

&

Pamela Jean George (1967-1995)

Three Indigenous Martyrs

Dossier

1 Frontispieces

23 Notorious I-IV

35 Psycho V-XII

51 Shadow of a Doubt XIII-XVI

65 Foreign Correspondent XVII-XXVI

83 Vertigo XXVII-XXX

95 Suspicion XXXI-XXXVI

109 Blackmail XXXVII-XL

119 Saboteur XLI-XLIV

129 The Birds XLV-XLVIII

141 Sabotage XLIX-LII

151 I Confess LIII-LVIII

167 Frenzy LIX-LXVIII

187 Backwords

FRONTISPIECES

For the Murdered & the Missing: A Spiritual

The best beloved of all things ... is Justice...
　　　　—Bahá u'lláh, *The Hidden Words*, I.2

Someone's guilty of a million crimes!
Blood on his hands, *Death* on his mind!
To send my sister away, away;
To put my mama in an unmarked grave.

Why she gotta be murdered?
Why she gotta go missing?
This land is hers, so I heard!
All the saints are insisting!

Someone's gotta sink in Hell and rot!
Dumped bones in bush or parking lot.
Disappeared my auntie, saw her die;
Exiled my daughter, served her *Misery*!

Why she gotta be missing?
Why she gotta be murdered?
Why I hear *Justice* hissing
Like a viper in a graveyard?

Someone's papa mapped a *Trail of Tears*!
Someone's son paved a *Highway of Tears*!
Why my sister gotta stumble down?
Why my mama gotta tumble down?

Why she gotta go missing?
Why she gotta be martyred?
Indigenous insisting,
"*Justice* for our massacred!"

Someone's flag looks like blood on snow!
Someone's *History*'s a damn *Crime* show!
To hurt my daughter so she weep;
To wound my auntie while she sleep.

Why she gotta be murdered?
Why she gotta go missing?
Martyred in mud, slush, *merde*—
From The Pas to Nipissing.

Someone's guilty of a million crimes—
From five centuries back, down to next time!
Ain't sorry to lil sister rape—
Or put my mama in her too-soon grave!

Why she gotta be murdered?
Why she gotta go missing?
Ain't all government alert
To crimes of commission?

Why don't Parliament just wail?
How can this Parliament fail?
Gotta have *Justice* insisting,
"No more murdered, no more missing!

"No more *Homicide, Suicide, Genocide*—
Those screaming words that none can hide!
No more *Trails* and *Highways of Tears*!
No more families cramming each a hearse!

"Time to put the guilty where they belong—
On trial, in jail, by the end of this song!"

Why she gotta go missing?
Why she gotta be murdered?
Indigenous insisting,
Justice for our massacred.

Justice for our massacred.
Justice, Justice, Justice, Justice,
Justice for our massacred.

Why she gotta go missing?
Why she gotta be murdered?

"J'Accuse...!": Diagnosis of an Imbroglio

Listen: Dread, panic, and horror are the great teasers, and tragic wisdom is our best chance in a dangerous world.
        —Gerald Vizenor, *Postindian Conversations*

I

The chronology of "For the Murdered and the Missing"?
Posted to my Parliamentary Poet Laureate website
in November 2017;
released in April 2019
on the Afro-Métis Nation CD, *Constitution*.

I composed that dirge because I want
assaults on Indigenous women to stop.
My reasons stem from home:
My mother, her mother, my aunts, my many cousins,
my daughter,
and "untolled" Indigenous Black—
Black Mi'kmaq and Africadians (Afro-Maritimers)—
and Afro-Métis women and girls—
have always been in *Jeopardy*:
Prey for men of all cultures, creeds, and complexions.

But my plangent chant—
a poem howled from out my heart—
was a blues jeremiad that no news agency
would report or broadcast—
whilst I was being defamed
in January 2020—
for allegedly caring more about *Poetry* and/or *Free Speech*
than I do about this Human Rights *Emergency*—
the documented atrocities of this flagrant *Genocide*
(a term I use *forensically*).

6

The blacklisting—*Repression*—of the ballad is telling.

As is the obscene—and outrageous—retailing
of the McCarthyite idea
(with maniacal kvetching)
that the editing or admiring of anyone's poetry
is tantamount to condoning the poet's crime(s).

To suggest that either *Poetry* (*Rhetoric*) or *Civil Rights*
must be *cancelled* to assert sincere *Solidarity*
with any community of righteous *Grievance*
is to posit a blatant *Tyranny*.

II

When Stephen Tyler Kummerfield, 20, and pal, Alex Ternowetsky, 19,
went tooling about Regina (SK) on April 17, 1995,
to hook (and left-hook) a sex-worker,
they succeeded only because Ternowetsky
secreted himself in their car trunk.
(No female *proxenetist* would enter a car with two johns.)
Once Ms. George, 28, was lured
into the spuriously solo-male auto,
she was wheeled to the boondocks of the burgh,
Ternowetsky popped from the trunk,
Rape was executed,
and then a mother of two girls
(and one predeceased son),
a Cree woman who liked to write verses,
was beaten to death—
and so drastically disfigured,
her mourners could view only her shuttered coffin.

III

Because Ternowetsky had plunked himself in the car trunk,
his cadaverous ruse hinted at plotted *Malice*,
and so both he and his accomplice,
could—should—have been life-sentenced for *First-Degree Murder*?
However, the trial judge—Ted Malone
(oft lambasted for alleged prejudicial, injudicious doublethink)—
ruled that because George was soliciting assignations,
she'd *consented* to sex acts the instant she'd *assented*
to get in the car,
and so she could not have been raped—*per se*.
And if she had not been—technically—raped,
nor had her violent demise been contemplated.
Thus, *Murder* got degraded to *Manslaughter*;
a pre-planned attack, downgraded to chance *Impulse*.

IV

At sentencing, out of potential jail time
of 7 to 10 to 25 years,
the two Caucasoid, settler lads—
Kummerfield (an ex-Crown minister's grandson)—
and Ternowetsky (a prof's scion)—
were sentenced to 6.5 years—
and served only 3.5—
I repeat, just 3.5 years—
in a New Brunswick, marshland-situated prison
where they could dodge Indigenous inmates—
the mainstay incarcerated of Saskatchewan—
who might have sought to mete out rough, jailhouse comeuppance
to two privileged, *bourgeois* fiends.

V

While transpired all this (the repulsive *Crime* against Ms. George
and the later, too-merciful penalty for the perps),
I was a junior prof at Duke University
in Durham, North Carolina,
toiling to establish African-Canadian literature as a scholarly field.
The news—all-American—dealt with blasting Serbia
and/or Al-Qaeda (at least trying to),
and did *not* cover yet *another* paleface, Canuck *Homicide*
against a Treaty 4 Cree.
I returned hesitantly to Canada to teach at McGill,
1998-99, when Ms. George's killers were still incarcerated.
I returned permanently (somewhat) to Canada to teach at U. of T.,
1999-2000, when the two murderers were awaiting release.
Neither offender had any existence pertinent to my *Consciousness*
or *Conscience*.

VI

When Kummerfield importuned me to read his verse
in February 2005, at a book launch in Toronto,
I said yes—as I have to *hundreds* of poets—
without a second thought—
over 40 years.
His surname did not scream *Rapist*;
nor was *Culpable Homicide* branded on his brow.
His poetry was edgy, gritty, but *Ausgezeichnet*.
I told him so, and we began to exchange verses
(a charity I've granted uncounted poet-comrades,
whose reciprocal edits have often "upped my game").
Soon, he requested that I intro his chapbook,
and I agreed—

so sassy and vivid was his Ginsberg vibe.
The skinny squib, *Man Bereft*, birthed in 2006,
and, as is standard for a novice,
garnered zero notice.
Then, Steve told me he was sundering his surname—
because it was "too ethnic."
(The history of authorship is rife with pseudonyms,
and, yes, Canucks tolerate a hierarchy of ethnicities.*)
Then the newly christened "Brown"
announced he was shunting off to Mexico,
that classic, expat locale for Beat *artistes*.
For the next 14 years,
we traded sporadic emails and poems;
I never felt the urge to check him out for a blood-stained past.
I rusticated in Cancún, México, in *septembre* 2015,
and Steve day-tripped to my resort hotel,
where, at supper, after imbibing much mescal,
he reared and spat at a German-parleying clan:
"I hate the fucking Germans for the Holocaust!"
"Relax," I urged.
His face flared purple in a *Paroxysm* I thought an anomaly.
Back to Ciudad de México, the next day, he jetted.
I last saw him—*there*—in February 2019.
With *amorissima* Giovanna at my side,
our impromptu trio recited *poesia ensemble*,
and saw released another paper-thin chapbook.
Its triadic authors: Clarke / Riccio / Brown.

* Cf. John Porter, *The Vertical Mosaic* (1965).

VII

So, I was astonished—rattled—flabbergasted
(*via* his email revelation in September 2019)—
to learn of Kummerfield-Brown's killing of Pamela George.

Disconsolate, discombobulated, disoriented,
I had to disown 14 years of discourse;
discontinue *Comity*, distance myself from *Amity*,
discourage any communication, discredit
a dishonest history, discard a *cucaracha*
Quasimodo, disbar his discrepant bonhomie.

VIII

Teaching Canadian (including Indigenous) Drama that Fall,
I told my students of my *Anguish* over the horrifying facts
(though I never mentioned S.K. by name).
I was trying to fathom a repellent *Crime*.

IX

Invited to Roma, Italia, to lecture, in November 2019,
I meditated publicly on artists who are dastards—
yes, even traitors.
I did not discuss S.K. by name, though I did relate
my agonizing over his lethal *Evil*.
Then, tasked to deliver the Woodrow Lloyd Lecture
at the University of Regina,
I'd yearned to critique "'Truth and Reconciliation' *versus*
The Murdered and the Missing:
Examining Indigenous Experiences of (In)Justice
in Four Saskatchewan Poets."

I do hold that the project of "Truth and Reconciliation"
is undermined by the *Failure* of
the squatter-class *Intelligentsia*—
predominantly Euro academics, jurists, journalists, and artists—
to acknowledge *their* murderous *Racism* and *Sexism*.
Would I have quoted Kummerfield/Brown's poetry
in that context?
Maybe. If *Research* had shown it to be instructive.
I'd not have gone to Regina to praise (or bury) a killer,
but to assess a body of poetry—
for what it could reveal about Saskatchewan intellectuals
and their perceptions of Indigenous women.

X

However, fearing that I'd seek to laud S.K.,
misinterpreters rejected all my assurances—
that I would dedicate the lecture to Pamela George,
that I would meet with elders,
that I would recite "For the Murdered and the Missing."
Only one worry was bruited:
Will you quote S.K.?
Soon, the parochial but ambitious Bonnie Allen—
a Sask-beat show-and-teller—
dialled my insular numerals,
demanding answers.
I explained, « I have to read and research.
Then, I can decide. »[*]
What she reported? « Maybe he will and maybe he won't. »
That *flippant* sound-bite—
clipped from a two-hour-long interview—
dog-whistled the bloggers
and pissed off bullshitters chomping at the bit.

---

[*] Throughout this book I use *guillemets* (« ») to represent invented speech or paraphrase.

XI

So, even though, "For the Murdered and the Missing"
had gone public two years before…,

breathless *Balderdash* pitched skilfully
an ugly, preposterous *Belief,*
one calculated to inculcate an Ass-Wipe Festival:

I.e., a regimen of *Spite*—
ineffaceably insidious,
barefacedly false,
and facetiously based

on my refusal to forecast to a reporter
(perhaps an Inquisitor journo, eh)
whether I'd quote a murderer's poetry
in an essay I'd yet to research and write.

And what was the basis for this sanctified *Gutlessness?*

I had befriended a Caucasian poet
who had slain an Indigenous woman,
something I knew nothing about—
a *Horror* inflicted years before he'd ever mailed me his poems;

yet, that fact got odiously exaggerated
into a colossal *Immorality*:

Were I to quote S.K.'s poetry,
I'd thus condone his vile *Infamy*.

(*Ironically*, however, it was not I,
but Allen's ballyhooed post,
that volleyed S.K.'s verse to potential thousands
of grousing browsers.)

A tabloid-sleazy gambit—*Guilt* by *Supposition*—crafted
a hullabaloo of scrofulous *Vilification*,
drafted an echo chamber looping *Vituperation*.

Though *prima facie* farcical,
the vacuous deduction proved conducive
to coaxing the hoaxed—
robust ignoramuses—
naïve crusaders—
witless illiterates—
(brains not too gracefully atrophied)—

to throaty, snarling *Hatred*.

So, I vacated my *Social Justice* preachment,
and I apologized *thrice*, *nationally*,
for any inadvertent *Pain*
triggered by my inability
to rehearse publicly
a non-existent essay.

Nonetheless, the Carpal-Tunnel-Vision Vicious
began, lickety-split, to clack, to click, to cluck…
To compose a tweeting, twittering star chamber—
to update Orwell, to hawk venom.

To say we must silence potential *Truth*-telling—
lest it seem « traumatic. »
Well, so are Holocaust testimony, Hiroshima autopsies, traumatic, eh?
To force *Change*.

(Thus, we value *Poetry* that *don't* compromise—
neither for critics nor for admirers.)

But I could not diagnose *Justice* or *Injustice*.[*]

I got expunged.
Poetry got nixed.

<u>Note: Paleface *Savagery* did *not*.</u>[**]

---

[*] The murderers, their deed, and their victim have been identified and described perennially through several decades. Thus, I do not change or omit their names or details. Besides, this work is a *Poem versus Silence* (and *Silencing*). *In atramento veritas*! The spirit of this riposte? Dylan in Manchester (UK), May 17, 1966: "Play fucking loud!"

[**] *"The palefaces are coming against us again, / for they are full of greed, lust and murder."* —Sky Dancer Louise Bernice Halfe, "tipiyawewisiw—ownership of one's self."

Trigger Warning: Message to the Grass Roots*

I remember P.E.T.'s 1969 "White Paper"—
its *Putsch* to bleach "Red People" into "White";
and to liquid-paper-out the ruddy history
of the settler-wrought, mass die-offs of toddlers and pupils
(due to smallpox, TB, bone-show *Starvation*, and/or capital *Battery*);
the extermination of the Beothuk;
the official assassination of Riel.

I know this because I, too, am a child of *Struggle*—
three-centuries *Worth*!
I'm born out of enslaved *homo sapiens* in Jamaica & Virginia—
Black people starved, whipped, shackled,
raped, segregated, lynched, jailed, executed!

How was Nova Scotia any better?
Coloured folk were kept incessantly illiterate—
jailhouse-prone, lethal-disease-prone,
worked-to-the-bone-prone, haggard and housed—
right next door to Mi'kmaq—
cos the Caucasoid squatters hated us both.

How "unintelligent" (sayeth Malcolm X) to say,
« We mustn't condemn the criminals!
Too hurtful is the accumulated blood! »

Why, if the *cancellaires* had been round during *Slavery*,
they would've pled, « It's too nerve-wracking
to register moms raped, daughters molested,
babes auctioned to top-dollar sadists. »
Holding a scented handkerchief to their noses,
they'd have banned the slave narratives!

---

* Cf. The pseudo-eponymous speech by Malcolm X, November 10, 1963.

Anyway, how do innocents stop being victims?
By victimizing others?

Or is it by scrutinizing atrocities—
those hordes of overseers and undertakers—
who disappear communes of corpses
out of *History*—
Wounded Knee, South Dakota,
& Batoche, Saskatchewan,
& Tulsa, Oklahoma—
as if massacres—plural—never happened?

Justice-demanding militants,
cleaving histories' pages,
should not be like finicky diners,
manipulating cutlery as if jewellers' tools,
morbidly focussed upon, hovering over,
a single cut of Wagyu beef,
but must consume and digest all,
to enable regurgitation of bloody facts,

and then act as clamorous guerillas—
to liberate the downpressed, to prosper *now* the exploited.

So, I embrace, I empathize with, Indigenous
brethren and sistren,
my natural allies.*

---

* See GEC, "The Constitution as Muse? Four Poets Respond (Tacitly) to the World-
View of *The British North America Act* (1867)" and the "Appendix: The Results of a
Sesquicentennial Constitutional Assembly—a Few Modest Amendments." *Review of
Constitutional Studies/Revue d'études constitutionnelles*. 22.3 (2017) [2018]: 289-324
& 325-328. In this paper, I propose situating "Indigeneity" at the *centre* of the
Constitution, thus displacing the Crown. See also, GEC, "Imagining the City of
Justice," the 7th Annual Lafontaine-Baldwin Lecture. Hosted by John Ralston Saul
and The Dominion Institute: Calgary, AB, March 10, 2006. In my talk, I advocated
the collection of 1% of property tax from all jurisdictions be transferred annually to

To vow *Outrage* versus outrages!

But disavow strident *Silencing*.

Silencing aligns one with Black Shirts and Brown Shirts,
Black Robes and White Hoods—
the "March on Rome" rather than the "March on Washington."

And this *Poem* is *versus Silence*...

First Nations. See also my Convocation Address, University of Alberta. Edmonton, Alberta, June 7, 2005. Therein I posited the Indigenous "recapture"—electorally—of the governance of Saskatchewan, achieving "self-government" by assuming all the constitutional powers of the province.

Postponed but Pertinent Elegy
for Geraldine Elizabeth Clarke, i.e., "The Original G.E.C."
(1939-2000)

Some say that I can say nothing about *Violence*
against Indigenous women…

But there you are, part-Cherokee definitely,
plausibly part-Mi'kmaq too,
and—*in your heart*—all Black,
limping,
one leg shorter than the other—
(due to Vitamin-D *Deficiency* imposed
by Royal Canuck scientists?).
So, may I not channel you who birth-canal'd me?

(Still, no elegy is ever sufficient!
Nor is the elegiac a narcotic!)

O you were ivory porcelain as breakable
as margarine is spreadable,
and your husband—my father—denied you
any symphonic *Happiness*;
yep, he tried to fetter an untamed dancer…

And you desired *Love*, but feared the lover.
(Or you desired the lover, but feared his *Love*.)

So audacious as an aria—
emphatically ritzy,
embodying a lady,
and blamelessly stunning,
every Black History Month saw you weighted down with valentines…

Such brown eyes—
umber so burnt as to be black!
And cream-coloured skin.

And you had the nerve to debut two daycares—
to earn your own bread,
instead of baking it.

Socialist, feminist, Alexa (McDonough) was your employee.

Yes, you limped—but never fell behind;
skittered high heels over slick, polished floors,
lingering perfume through the air.

Your savvy laughter embellished all,
yet was pugnacious enough
to knock the Queen of England off her throne.

(You'd giggle, jiggle, earthquakingly,
while tossing back your curls—
like a rebel hurling a Molotov cocktail!)

My father—your husband—thought bullish fists
could cow you—
go pow-pow-pow, thuggish:
and I, a boy, witnessed the bruises, the welts, the blood.

But you fled—busted out of—his P4W:

To have toasted raisin bread, sunny with butter,
marinée'd in cinnamon;
or let Coca-Cola and Cheezies stand in occasionally
for Champagne and caviar;

to savour crushed turnip with cream and salt;
to relish wine and rye bread and Dijon mustard and smoked meat;
to ogle AVON brochures
gussied up by Midsummer-Night's-Dream-variety Shakespeare;
to mix T.S. Eliot with *Tia Maria*…

Yes, you overpampered brutes and clods,
men who snickered into the booze you paid for.
To keep their love, you practiced the discipline of lies—
Espionage borrowed from *True Confessions*.
Until too much became too much,
and you'd pack up, and they were left kneeling, weeping.

A fashionista Sandinista—
no wonder,
your casket, Mom,
is really a jewellery box.

No wonder,
all diamonds fall dull—
absent your enlightening *Beauty*…

Thus, I bear witness to *Treasure*—
despite all opposing *Battery*.

NOTORIOUS

I.

Dissembling radio, rankling decibels, cranked syllables,
rancorous, I heard,
while trembling snow descanted,
slanting dawn,
the Plains-speaking Bonnie Allen—
professional, not cantankerous—
but sounding—*to me*—piqued, cranky—
wreaked absurdist, havocking words?

I mean, it was so weird to be found—
a hapless felon—I
(and well outside a SAVAK confessional)!

So, how could I, *The Notorious G.E.C.*,
speak to Saskatchewan's inglorious, corpse-bloated,
blood-leaking *History*?

An *arrogant* prof,
who just might dissect
a Caucasian killer in a lecture on *Race*-complected *Femicide*,
I was now *Verboten*:
My speech crossed out; the concepts crucified.

Figured now was signal *Disdain*, an *Arraignment*:
The gist? A sniggering prank?!!

Was thus the frank disgrace, the vain *Dummkopf*—
I—seared, singed, blackened—
Day 2 of 20/20—
vingt-vingt—
Year of the Rat (Fink)—
in stereo cacophonous?

« Clarke might quote the ex-con's *Poesy*—
or maybe not. »

Syllables swollen to loco decibels canted—
sarcophagus-hollow:

He's a poet who values Poetry *more than* Silence...

II.

What is left for me to do in *Poetry* save confess?

Did or did not the radio dissemble?

Wasn't I Cinna the Poet,
who, confused for Cinna the Conspirator
(br'er to Shakespeare's Brutus
in twirling and swirling Czar Julius
that original "bloody Caesar"),
the carelessly vengeful, Roman mob shredded,
cannibalized, trunk and trembling limbs?

I confess I befriended a bard who—
one of two rhyming punks—
annulled pell-mell—hellishly—
Ms. Pamela Jean George—
parfit, *gentil*, splendid, a poet—
in April 1995,
in dirty, bone-crushing Regina,
in the crimson slush of its outskirts...

One disgorged at breakfast,
« I killed an Indian chick. »
No forgery.

One decade later,
at his pleading, I read verses
all seedy cussin and heady *Decadence*—
the nervy imagery, starkly *Grand-Guignol*-dark.
His admission? His omission of *Homicide*.

(His omission? His admission of *Homicide*.)

So, I knew zilch of his notorious, crunching *Butchery*—
the bilge and belch of his punch-drunk *Putsch*,
the *Pandemonium* of his *mater* ambush,
his milquetoast-ghost-white face spunking lies.

III.

I'd just risen—*café-au-lait* Nosferatu—out my basement
when execrable decibels sabotaged—
smeared fallaciously—sideswiped—my visage…

Wasn't the radio defecating *Disdain*—
feces flooding my ear canals
(feces also framing my screened mugshot)—
because I'd refused to spell out—
whether I'd quote a blood-coated poet?

Wasn't I only blurting speech "[causing] hurt"—
cautioned Regina U.'s Prez Timmons—
impressive spittle belittling lips?

Wasn't I only grinding "salt in wounds"?
Sneered smart-aleck Heather Mallick—
airing icky *Malice*, farting *Merde* and *Dreck*—
heckling, fecklessly, « Why didn't you query:
"Have ya ever murdered anyone?"
Before ya checked out the poseur's *Poesy*?!! »

Wasn't I "Guilty by association," as attested Allen,
telephoning in that *koan* (公案)—
as if I'd leagued with clouting louts, acted
the blood-extracting felon…

Moi-même, j'étais la bête noire de la Tour d'ivoire!

Overnight, I was notorious!
Didn't screens and lungs just screech?!!

(Hurled my way now were humongous stink bombs!)

Nicotine'd tongues,
plungering smutty ashtrays and skanky bottles,
keening after *Fiasco*,
furious—urged my *Arraignment*:

He's a poet who values Poetry *more than* Silence...

IV.

After New Year's Eve-loud swank with the *Exile* crowd,
tucking into a roast suckling pig, giggling,
grinning, "cin-cinning" the redoubled bubbly,
swigging the light-spanked toasts to 2020,

I was just ascending—sable—from my basement,
at dawn of Day 2—
when ribald syllables began soiling the airwaves,
schlepping thud-thud into roiled ears,
the grime and dirt uncoiling personal *Defamation*
out the radio—
unconstrained contaminant—
the airwaves feculent, soiled,
each banal vocable a grave,
unconstrained contaminant—
pitilessly defacing *moi*—the gargoyle-prefaced airwaves…

Suddenly, I was tripped, fallen, vulnerable—
and my verses accursed and unviable.

The radio kept venting a tinny voice
(a reporter who exaggerates her *t*'s—
a dental detonated to close a wheeze):
"News" no better than tittering noise…

Next, I eyed my mug, slanted—
WANTED—postered—
beside the milquetoast thug—
Janus-faced Caligula or bug-eyed Dracula…
Broadcast I was side-by-side—
the psycho and his *notorious* sidekick:
As if my shtick were also *Homicide*.

*

On the airwaves settled the grave mud—
the showering dirt thud-thudding:
« Clarke won't say what he'll say
in a lecture he hasn't written… »

PSYCHO

V.

When Steve (Greek for *Laurel wreath* or *crown*)
Kummerfield
(German for *Field of Sorrow*)—
grandson of a leftist *Honourable*
(sprout from our rabble)—
and Alex Ternowetsky—
(offshoot of a prof)—

both lugs
(each lad a type of psycho)—

replayed Hernán Cortés
and Kit Columbus—
to club down an "Indian" (again),
to rub out a "squaw,"

I was professoring in No'th Ca'lina,
where flag-waving (grave-digging), TV news
showcased slo-mo views of US ("our") cruise
missiles aimin to degrade—maim—Belgrade (Serbia).

News outta *Dead Zone* Saskatchewan?
Stateside, there'd be broadcast none!

Naturally, in 1998, I deafeningly heard
of the East Texas lynching—epic—of James Byrd—
chained at the ankles and dragged behind a speeding
flivver, his body slivered apart unto his septic beheading.

*

Still, "Guilt by association" prefaced my networked *Shame*:
Was I not as *prima facie* sinful as Cinna the Poet
(who, confused for an assassin of Caesar, *via Conspiracy*,
got ripped apart as easily as pages of tyro *Poetry*)?

VI.

The ditch squelched gooey; mud belched
fractures, busted skull, where Steve, psycho—
laurel-wreathed lug fielding *Sorrow*
(what his germane surname divulges)—
Alex-aided and Alex-abetted—
avalanched upon a honey-fleshed being,
on that snow-pearled April night,
whelping stains as winds whirled, walloped…

*

I was down in No'th Ca'lina,
watchin Mur-ka work o'er Sur-be-ah,
and so I be oblivious to yet *another* invidious,
SasKKKatchewan*-squatter vicious
Slaughter of yet *another*
Indigenous mother and daughter.

*

25 years on, some were thinking I'd brood
that a poet's ink scours off a mother's blood
slopping pitiless fists…
But such isn't—and wasn't—who I avowedly *is*.

*

(I's part-Cherokee, prob'ly part-Mi'kmaq,
an Afro-Métis, brown-black,
and never stomped down no woman—or poetess.)

---

* "Canada's Alabama"—Peter Gzowski (*Maclean's*, July 6, 1963).

VII.

I sensed scathing *Anathema* emanate out the radio.
Defecate a crescendo of *Innuendo. Merde*!

Acrimony excreted out the radio!
Nixonian expletives, undeleted, lousing up stereo:

« Why won't the ex-Parliamentary Poet Laureate
say what he will say
in a lecture he has not written? »

*

Day 2—2020—*Année du* Ratso—
played out the *Regina (Mephisto) Manifesto*
(a xylophone of bone and gristle):
Heard I slurry syllables
in unspooling decibels,
drooling my *Guilt,*
although it be two Caucasoid psycho
cowboys, Western Front sodbusters,
who tricked—blinkered—hoodwinked
good, gentle Ms. George—
(a striving poetess of *maybe* sugared georgics)—
cos unblinking Alex hunkered in a car trunk,
while slick Steve whirled the wheel
so Pamela—*Pan Miel* (*All Honey*)
(and that sweet, bardic name descendeth from poet Philip Sidney)—
wouldn't know, didn't know,
she'd be grappling with doubled *Lustmord*:
Two guys—defalcators—scowling, their snake eyes,

owlish, all the April night under stars,
as they whaled upon the quailing *mater*…
(*Inculpatory* their calipers, their scalpels, their rebar.)

*

At dawn, one psycho joked, « Killed an Indian chick. »[*]

---

[*] On 11 May, 1963, nine white worthies of Glaslyn (SK) slew—lynched—Allan
Thomas, a Saulteaux. They shrugged. Their victim? "Just an Indian." Hear the echo?

41

VIII.

The white-boy, good-ole-boy, Proud Boy—
rough riders, Odin Soldiers, stampeders—
every Ku Klux Klan, Boogaloo psycho—
had always sickled down, pell-mell, grassland belles.
Métis and Cree—
whether girls or great-grandmas;*

next, would parade scarlet on N.W.M.P. sables—
or slink behind R.C.M.P. desks
(or perhaps join the C.R.A.P.,
their think-tanking *Justice* downright fickle)—

or hunker, sunk, in car trunks—
to give a gal *epistaxis*
(or deliver dudes *rigor mortis*—
via Saskatoon "starlight tours"—
to taxi and force a Cree *mec*—
far from domestic *Warmth*—
into sub-zero, subversive temperatures,
prompting frigid *Rigidity*)—

to deform *territoire* into *film noir*.

Lookit! There be *Wisdom* in *Terror*!
(The Caucasoid eyes of Conrad's Kurtz fearing his mirror.)

*

Beneath her killers, she fell quiet.
Only in her obit could she breathe, titular.

---

* Regard "the contempt in which the Indian [sic] women are held by Saskatchewan whites."—Peter Gzowski (*Maclean's*, July 6, 1963).

IX.

Years on, monthly, Steve slobbered tequila—
his eye-sealing sobbing aping *Feeling*.
But *Remorse* was so much touchy-feely junk:
Tears glommed in gobs, but each just gunk.

He'd donkey-punched, rabbit-punched, sucker-punched,
a nourishing *mater* and a flourishing poet
into her death-bed ditch—a muddy, gravel mash.

(Felled like Helen Betty Osborne; like Anna Mae Aquash.)

No, not *he*, he lied, but another—
had wrought intracranial hemorrhage,
vertebral fracture;
brought blunt-force, bunched hands
unto the occiput;
no, not *he*, but someone else
(throbbing poisons in his psycho pulse)—
had forged, had wrought, Ms. George's unredacted *blut*.

*

Yet, I was (as in Red-Scares archaic) "Guilty by association,"
meditated the Press, *eupneic*—nay, huffing—
as if I jolly well could be Golliwog,
deserving my stuffing kicked out—plus *Defamation*.

Dull screens smeared my face with smog,
ejaculated my name along with phlegm.

So painstaking the yuk-yuk muckraking…
The lobbed tirades…

Flummoxing.

X.

A P-h-D guttersnipe,
not quite a lynchee of hemophiliac type,
I stood as blackly accused
as any blackguard…

Or so burred that guttural *Insinuation, Innuendo,*
blurring air waves and TV screens—
with no diminuendo—
for 72 hours… Recurring… *Excommunication… Spleen.*

*

But two plutocratic punks—
in a *Pugilism* punitive as primitive *Zoology*—
after brunching and lunching on booze—
the colleged bachelors—their punches contrapuntal,
their blows ballistic—
faltered a balladeer, her breath halting—
she, martyred, blighted.

But rubbed I "salt in wounds," jeered Heather Mallick, indignant.
I was—ignominiously—"a general honours magnet,"
a suspect magnate of trophies, medals, prizes?

(*Maybe* a too breezily flippant or easily malignant a figure,
somehow slipping the *Stereotype*-snagging dragnet?
My laurels just capped clip-on, Sambo disguises?!!)

*

But wasn't it the Caucasoid cowboys who'd condoned

fisticuffs, who were toughs—
exhibiting the pale demeanour of bones?

Didn't Steve—swinish—play psycho—
Caligula Siamesed with *Dracula*?

(Is not "Redskin" murder the redneck bio?)

XI.

A phone(y) interview framed my "crime"?
"Guilt by association."

My copper face—a dummy's sopped in silver rime—
screened with voice-overs of tom-tom respiration,
just had to inspire supersized, vulgar *Ire*!

In stereo and in Day-Glo, flared yellow, piss-groggy *Journalism*,
hog-snorts flagging me as th'accomplice,
slagging me before hang-em-high, virtual lynchers,
the swaggering nags, the campus-pompous…

*

None other than twin sicko, psycho chums
swirled a hurricane of dexterous jabs, sinister stabs.
To bash and lather *via* leather knuckles,
plus truculent boots, also smutching.

(Hear the cracking substance that's springtime ice.)

Nunc pro tunc, nunc pro tunc
(as right now as it was back then—always);
all undone—three belt buckles:
The *demoiselle* in the ditch, face-down;
two Rippers ogling, watching
(bruised be their knuckles).

*

Me? I muster with "hostiles" as every ex-slave does.
Yet, never once did I decree
Poetry as immune
to screams, to weeping, to *Contumely*…

No, to Sky Dancer—and Poundmaker—I attune.

XII.

Did Steve and Alex differ from squatter psycho forebears—
fanatics engineering the *Misanthropocene*—
steering "Indians" to give up (on) their messiahs?

Weren't they all Euro-trash Conquistadors—buccaneers,
preaching, « To fuck is to open a coffin! »

So what tears can palliate—soften—obscene
dying before serene, indifferent justices, stodgy,
foreseeing only another "dodgy" *mater* body-bagged—
and her ghost post-mortem slagged?

*

Missing intolerably is the possible
hint of rosy, floral notes backed with wild mint,
her *Self*—mellow as vanilla or spring-bank clover—
the spice—mild bergamot—some tea on her tongue.

Yes: There'd been solicitous *Toil* for staples—
to stock up on milk, eggs, bread, whatnots, extras—
to keep full the table, the cupboard, the fridge…

How else to make a crib a type of Sistine Chapel?
(And hadn't *Saint* Mary Magdalen sometimes peddled her ass?
And hadn't even that *proxenetist* found *Salvage*?)

*

Beautiful as a Modigliani,
Ms. George tumbled—sprawled—
before unbearable headlights:
A car became a shaking hearse…

SHADOW OF A DOUBT

XIII.

Always was mine blood-poisoning poetry! Reputedly:
It was beautiful *Poesy*—if out a dutifully disputed pen.
(Black ink silhouetting—ferociously—crimson—
a jetting spree.)

There had been cocky, Caucasoid,
clamorous thuds clambering over,
hammering down, voiding
a woman, no more ever a lover—

nor mother, nor poet-cowgirl of the rodeo…
But I was too much an Ivory Tower Negro—
Negroid—thus "Afro-Métis" (so implausible)—
to guillotine *Injustice*. It just weren't possible.

*

A honey-sweet *mater* had gone dramatically dead;
yet, her slayers won excuse almost axiomatically:
« Too much *Southern Comfort* had sloshed each boy's head! »

Thus a pale jurist—judicious—tut-tutted:
« George was a prostitute,
thereby impervious to *Rape*, eh? »

No shadow of a doubt!

Bammed—jolt after jolt—the posthumous blows of *Slander*,
judge and defence cavilling at the muted victim—
her *Murder* rendered almost moot as *Blame* gavelled.

(What does a corpse risk,
save *Indignity?*)

Wasn't the court rubbing malicious salt
in the body-in-the-ditch-in-the-heather wounds,
to let a killer soon salt-and-lime his tequila?

XIV.

Didn't the *mater*'s *Assassination* resemble classical Actaeon,
harried and hobbled, then gobbled by his own hounds?
(Playing Cinna the Poet, watch Chaplin pratfall, bludgeoned.)

Witness the screeching darkness of a heather outside Regina,
the skittering indigo green of a jittery April field, sorrowful,
thawing into muck;

see Alex, scruffy, bellicose, exiting a trunk, unhitched.
Hear the morbid bitching of gavels and settler creeds!
Eye the ruddy petals maculating gravel and weeds...

Hear morally comatose, a jurist's twitchy syllables, gabbled—
his decibels—in high dudgeon—judge *faux* a « Jezebel »...
(How else to mute a corpse, keep killers at large,

if not by electing *Slander* over the autopsy?)

No shadow of a doubt!

*

Quarter-century after, my home phone jangled *Consternation*.
I audited a histrionic, distorted *Condemnation*:
My platonic *Guilt*—gaudy—angled in sporting breaths!

Soon, my unsaid lecture got impeached in speech whitey-white!
Then came moseying the mint-condition, yellow newsprint—
cozy letters as black as burnt-over land, the buried deaths,*

---

* Cf. "Untolled" thousands of children clumped in unmarked graves at numerous,
forced *Assimilation* (culturally genocidal) "schools."

so a screen could wash yellow like piss-gilded snow,
my niggered, narcissus self get mangled stigmatically—
cos I couldn't say what I'd quote cos I didn't yet know.

XV.

His pond'rous Honour chose to try
A mother broke like pottery—
Her blood dark but buttery...
To maul her in the mortuary?

A squalid, paleface coterie
Had elected to try,
Not *Murder*, but *Sluttery*:
Tongues perfected *Battery*.

The accused snagged a lottery!
Latin words could shadow *Flattery*?
A daughter had died of *Sluttery*,
Not a plague of fungal *Battery*.

Only the Mad Hattery
Of a squatter court could try
A corpse for *Sluttery*,
Vaunt *Southern Comfort* as *Poetry*.

Whose tears were merely watery?
That Jurassic coterie—
Students of classic *Poetry*—
Whose lines lyric *Battery*!

A citizen's blood is glittery
In the ditch, her breath jittery.
The Milky Way turns buttery,
As she—martyr—flutters into *Poetry*.

I have no else way to try
Latinate voices—fluttery—
In a squatter-court Mad Hattery—
Where the Muse is murdered *Poetry*.

No shadow of a doubt!

XVI.

Blobs of blood amid globs of snow, gobs of muck,
the scraping videotape unwound in white-noise din;
close-up on wounds that gloves, boots, knuckles, struck,
smucking—desecrating—a Cree woman's skin.

Two clodhopper Prairie Munsters deigned to say—
that, after cracking a cold case of *Southern Comfort* sludge,
their paired brace had bracketed their prey:
Thus, Ms. George sustained *Injury* that made her spudge

a smudging Parma-violet, stains bludgeoning her purse...
The twain accused—buff as Popeye on spinach—
gesticulated testily, huffed, « She was no worse
for wear when we'd left her, slobbering, in a ditch.

Face-down. Either the blameless elements
or a nameless passerby struck the *coup de grâce*: Black-ice hard!
Of *Murder*, we declare our *Innocence*! »

(Yet, her visage—marred—now wronged her ID card.)

Serving but 3.5 years of 6.5 sentenced
(less than the usual 8 or 12 or 25),
honky S.K. slipped soon his monkey-bars, quick to thrive
(just as I became Big Smoke residenced)—

the bard slithered free his monastic cell—
5 years *before* scrumming (dummy) me to peruse
his bluesy, cardio-vascular verses, his odd *Godspell*—
a reborn, hoser hustler, his slumming rhythms woozy...

No shadow of a doubt.

*

Blushing had been the rushing blows—
until a mom mirrored crushed rubbish.

[Rupture: A Trial Post-Mortem.]

Within this aura of Beauty
an ugliness intrudes…
> —Hardial Bains, *Thinking About the Sixties: 1960-1967*

Originally, was she apprehensive?
The dual hulks mimic'd the bulk of cash registers,
so she'd nixed—deep-sixed—"the date,"
til seemingly only a singular chuckled his engine back.

Had she found most palefaces unerringly similar—
unbelievably malicious, abjectly mendacious,
and profoundly unhygienic?
Lechery dependent on *Treachery*,
if not *Bribery*?

(Some dirt escapes rinsing.)

Preachers, politicos, teachers, "simple serpents"—
all em Bible and *Law*-book thumpers—
blurting fecal trumps
(tiresome as flies hounding dung):

Gee whiz, were any of em
anything other than demonic thingabobs?
They're not so much born
as expelled—shat out—from the womb?

Are the Prairie *zwiebacks* ("crackers") hordes
of ruthlessly gluttonous hog-guts
(priapic as billy clubs);
swinish eyes with monocles;
Kaputt faces with *Silly Putty* grimaces?

Could one sight, at the bungled trial,
dough-pudgy clerks—
and/or the defendants
(plaster striving to pose as marble)—
Drs. Worse and Worse—
appallingly pallid,
doubling as ghouls,
standing in as gargoyles;
each one a *furunculus* on the eyeball;
each one belonging in a penal colony;
their hearts rancid,
their emotions utterly ceremonial?

Was the judge unbothered by unzipped viscera?
Decomposing painfully. In plain sight.

Was the killing field that night Utopia, not Hades?
Was his face a crust of whitewashed *papier-mâché*?

Were not the tag-team rapists
dreaming to snuff their mothers—
every female—
like every flame?

(Because those who give birth,
who nurture life,
also subject the new being
to a death sentence?)

No shadow of a doubt?

Witness the *Damnatio Memoriae.*

Gravedigger aroma of lilies and violets.
That candid stench.

(I have no else way to try
Battery shattering *Poetry*.)

FOREIGN
CORRESPONDENT

XVII.

Materialized a *Star-Trek*-teleported phantasm—
Steve—all plastic speech, alabaster ectoplasm—
all sly, sporting parley—
at my downtown, Hogtown, Soul-Gospel Concert, Launch
Party—
for *George & Rue*,
my *True Crime* novel bout my hanged back-to-back,
Injun-Nigger killer-cousins, flung down the flue.
(Yipper:* Cue the black-comic laugh track...)

*

Maybe Steve believed it no prophetic forgery—
that curious, nomenclature *Imagery*
tic-tac-toe-ing George Albert Hamilton,
Afro-Métis executed for *Murder*;
Pamela Jean George,
Kummerfield's Cree victim;
and George Elliott Clarke,
Afro-Métis wraith faithfully limning murders...

Why not?
Being the virtuoso behind *Execution Poems*,
didn't I squat in the grotto of jingoistic *Elegy*?
Void of all *Virtue*?

*

---

* 1980s Kitchener-Waterloo (Ontario) slang for *Yes*.

That premier confab in Toronto
(a decade after Steve's insidious crime)
was echoed in a second decade's time—
by a second gab session in Mexico.

In between, I was Steve's foreign correspondent.
(Of how invidious that post was, I bleed innocent.)

La chienlit,
c'est lui.

XVIII.

What slick hocus-pocus! Quick, the hind name became "Brown";
he'd sloughed off his mugshot alias—
like pus off a wound—
and vamoosed, loco; *hasta-la-vista*'d his locus to Mexico…

German for *Sorrowful, Pathetic*—
Kummerfield—as the slumming bard had been known
got painted over *Kahlúa*-brown…
Steve's expound? *Kummerfield*'s "sound" be « Too ethnic… »*
Unpleasant to pasty-faced publishers—
and too-peasant-like for Anglo editors!

*

Soon came racing my way—Steve's multiple tracings
of racy *Howl*, of culpable *On the Road*, of ersatz Miller,
of Ferlinghetti—Ginsberg—Jones/Baraka—Kerouac—
Creeley/Corso, Dylan B/W Villon,
Beat poets—
their burp guns' splattered or spattered letters, jetty—
rat-a-tat-tatting—
tattling—
of the Corso Italia cut with Casablanca—
Soho back-alleys gelling—*giallo*—in Chicago—
or Harlem transmogrified by hashish
(due to Negro pornocrats plying the Vice Squad with baksheesh).
I ferreted out rat-tailed Billy Burroughs playing Billy Tell

---

* For S.K. to shift his surname did not strike me as a criminal's gambit, but rather as
an attempt to heighten the chance of publication and/or to preserve privacy. The
example of the Prairie-based Canuck novelist Freddy Philip Grove (*né* Felix Paul
Greve), also German in background (like—I guess—Kummerfield—but also an ex-
con), would have been readily available to S.K. Not to mention those of Joey Conrad
and—*ahem*—Georgie Eliot…

with his touchy-feely conjoint—Saint Joan—
the brain-eviscerating bullet translating into ink—hellish,
dripping (like Joan falling, prone)—
onto yellowed newspapers extra-gilt with cat-piss…
I eyed a Mexico of erotic cartoons, bona fide narcotics,
plus *Coitus*—syphilitic pus oozing, pelvic as Elvis…
Treponema as infectious as soap operas.

Inscrutably, I became a pariah poet,
a carious poet, indubitably: This foreign correspondent…

XIX.

Introduced I Steve's chapbook, *Man Bereft* (m.m.v.i.)…

A treat were his evasive conceits, abrasive as *Deceit*,
his hoody'd, neighbourhood stalkings,
talking "psychogeographical," hoodoo blues,
slouched over turntable voodoo beats.
His woozy, psycho bleats,
cognitively smoggy.

Perverse verses bounced riffs off Bobcat's
"Just Like Tom Thumb's Blues"—
cataloguing Lolitas, *panochitas*, *mamacitas*—
teeter-tottering on forget-me-not high heels—
spandex starbursting glitter o'er their crotches…
Spellbound as if by a contact spliff,
si, I was gaga for this urbane banter, this spiel—
ig'orant bout a *mater* avalanched into drainage…

*

I praised good poetry by a bad man.
I wasn't whitewashing *Bloodshed*.
I was trying to advise a poet—
not help him scrub up as sparkly as Liberace.

*

What's left for lost, nigger me to do in *Poetry*
but bleat ma plural *mea culpa*?

Yipper, I was Steve's foreign correspondent.

XX.

Was Sis George Florentine honey-and-milk,
clementine-sweet, adamantine silk—
multipara
and *sans pareil*?

I cannot know or say.

But doesn't *Eulogy* enact a sort of Henri Rousseau
softening—*via* pastel?
Thus, the Court's *Sabotage* of *Personality*
was gratuitously whimsical:
Why rob the slain of the customary, grace-note halo?

Yet, I do not romanticize.
I do not eulogize.

Her life was terminated
by two middle-class germs.

And she was discounted by a jurist.
(Did words flake—scabrous eczema—
off his tongue?)

And then I humoured a Club Fed partisan's natter—
convoluted numbers, wheezed like emphysema—
I didn't know grew out of contusions, wounds, tumors,
sprouted by white-fist blood-splatter;

so, the *giallo* journalists, exploiting *Grief*,
could exploit—beyond *Belief*—*Rage*, so adroitly:

To malign my bad self, my stinking prayers,
cos I'd been Steve's foreign correspondent...

XXI.

My foreign correspondent's pages? Fitful, fretful guitar—
startled strings yowling like operatic, Argento cats,
musical notes as strident as skunk perfume,
or screams that mushroom
outta salt rubbed in wounds? (I recall Mallick.)
Or due to a shiv thrust into anyone vaguely chivalric?

[Yet, intriguing was Steve's literalizing of the Italian word *stanza*,
effected by erecting his verses in rectangular, vertical "boxes,"
sometimes connected by looping, arrow-headed lines,
but each featuring different, aberrant narratives
(some confected, some hoaxes),
yet often running concurrently—
until something gives.]

*

I could smell the acrid waltzes
of pen and ink salsa-ing paper,
frisking plated sheets briskly;
I could audit the dancing squawks of pencils
(*lead chalk* that bumps off a sonnet)—
copying the biblical scowl of a *Tribulation* poet
in the Satan-heroic mode of Milton!

(Did I applaud a gringo *Dégringolade*—
a low-down Lowry avowing volcanic ballad?)

*

True. Each poem surfed invisible (or illegible) scum.
His frontal lobotomy was the tequila bottle in front of him.

XXII.

A decade after two knaves, craven, scourged Ms. George,
forging her into a cadaver,
purging her soul *via* a hand-over-fist fusillade,

Steve was sauntering *infra dig* haunts
all about Colonia Roma (in Mexico City—
its Manueline architecture vaunting Neo-Gothic *Coma*—
plus "Art Nouveau and Neo-Classical abodes"—
as enthuses the Wikipedia palaver)—

after having schemed to fetch bloody stigmata—
pitiless—upon ruddy pigmentation—

and now had my name booked on his cover—
not yet rebuked as "inappropriate."

*

If only I'd only been a foreign correspondent!
A token poet!
Not a newfangled—if accidental—Cinna!

But too late to stymie alleged "Guilt by association"—
the banal, sloganeering oration channelled
(byline—bonny Allen)…

That transparent piss hissing out the phone—
searing my ears. I was *that* Ivory Tower nigger.
That drat public figure.
That Phoney.

Fallen.

XXIII.

After a *decad* of poems shuttled back and forth—
Steve scuttled—posted—to Cancún
(as a ghostly coon can)—
September (M.M.X.V.), but did not disgorge
Ms. George's cadaver—
cantilevered into the boot of his brain—
while shooting tequila & fluting mescal palaver.
Our second meet—*pace* ten years? A refrain.

And zealous was his sopping palate at the resort *ravintola*:
Til eavesdropped we on tourists swaggering German decibels—
all those bopping, obstreperous, or staggering syllables—
and, from our table, Steve reared hind legs—
uncaverned—ungovernable (like jazz out of NOLA),
and, upchucking *Fury*
at the *Deutschland* clan (steeped in their kegs),
struck air with irrevocable, vocal *Injury*—
"I hate the fucking Germans for the Holocaust!"

Steve's impetuous *Irritation*, incorruptible *Hatred*,
waiters and diners ignored. (Wasn't he just a gringo, lost?)
But I acted as his calming, foreign correspondent…
(About his own *Crime*, I was yet innocent.)

So we hugged—and next he was gone—
after bugging out
(slugging the table after ceviche got chugged)—
back to Mexico City. The perfectly unknown (to me) ex-con.

*

Was he susceptible to that desperate *Inspiration, Grief?*
Did his eyes spike with overcast tears
like the blinding, grey tears—striking—*grisaille*—
the eyes of Ms. George's survivors?
Well, never did his verses record *Remorse*...
Nor damn the perverse crimes of *racaille*!
All got papered over by white-sheeting rime—
a rapacious (if surreptitious) I-I-I-I—
even if each edgy page turned
pledged a new leaf.

XXIV.

There ain't nuttin fo me to do in *Poesy* but confess…

I read about blowtorch winds incinerating dusty avenues—
skulls of white sugar, unorthodox sweets—
a subhuman economy of subterranean *Torture*—
offed bees who didn't call ya honey—
garter snakes intruding into garter belts—
red nail polish wielding fatally a silvery straight-razor—
rotting lungs vomiting a trinity of Absinthe, Bacco, Cocaine—
the Wow and Whoopee of skin—
bones handcuffed—clamped—to muscles and nerves—
crotches oozing molasses while mouths are slopping brine—
Sex that's all Lollapalooza somersaults—
Barbie dolls in *Lego*-block-like quandary positions—
cologned demons staging crucifixion championships—
a first-rate "Second Coming"—
prudential cooing and improvident sighing—
a saxophone spraying song in violet puffs
(ugh! scruffy, ejaculatory blues)—
a tinsel-skinny woman reeking a big-money smell—
soccer moms, cheerleaders, poodle-strolling pimps—
banjos shaped like the Big Dipper—
an ideology of government bullet-holes in student dissidents—
exaggerated switchblades shiny and slithery as alligator shoes—
Miles Davis bebop trumpet popping Dylan Thomas dentals—
the sun as an unmatched burst of flame latched to a match—
beached white silk bleaching to red meat—
Rotwelsch (German slang) become soundtrack to slasher *gialli*—
that musky, sauna haze of Valentine's Day night—
anemone-pallid stars sparking honeyed ballads outta bars—
disembarked, cruise-ship Romans Shanghai'd in Colonia Roma:

Split-level stanzas, rectangles or squares—
divulged all the muscular sunlight,
disturbances of crepuscular gunfire,
or brown madams pissing in parkland briars, *et cetera*.

*

Steve of the prevaricating tongue and quirky, squiggly lips,
working my foreign correspondent leaves and poetic tips!

XXV.

Eventually, Regina's Sleuths sussed out that Steve Brown
was actually Steve *Worrisome* or *Sorrowful*
(*Kummerfield* being a German surmise)—
he, who—with his comrade in bad-assery—
had so bashed and defaced their prey—
her funeral witnessed a locked-tight coffin.

Face the facts: Reliably *Establishment*—
two pale squirts of ruling—squatter—class Saskatchewan—
had dashed—mangled (bloodied)—a brown citizen—
who liked crafts, drawing, and to craft or drawdown poems.

Dry-cleaned, dapper—tuxedo'd in the court—
Murder and *Rape*
(cf. Titus Andronicus)
comported themselves as if each were a pampered day camper
gone astray.

*

But now the Trackers turned up Steve
« cavorting with a brown man »—
the ex-Poet Laureate:
That sporting dunderhead, blundering *moi*!

Swirled now a lasso, a lariat,
a lynch-mob* noose (a halo ignited by Satan)…

*

---

* Or "demagogic populists"? See Harry C. Boyte, *Academic Matters* (Spring 2017),
p. 27.

Only now did my foreign correspondent blurt,
« I hurt—I mean, I slew—an Indigenous woman. »

September 20, 2019, his confess detonated drone-like
in my ears: Breath sagged; heart burned to bone.

What's left for me to do in *Poetry*, but confess?
I hadn't seen the demon exiting the car trunk…

XXVI.

Steve's jaws dumped scraps, clumps, pap—
pure *Dreck, Invective, Deflection.*
« I thought you knew [I was a murderer], »
prevaricated that harlequin-and-gravedigger,
then blubbered about being an artist-martyr,
slobbering the super-duper tears of a funeral parlour director...

(But George's bio *his* autobio desecrates.)

*

But he'd eradicated—enacted the subtraction of—
a woman of floral and honeyed undertones—
while he, too-quick sprung, quickly kicked back,
scarfing tacos and quaffing tequila,
intoning epileptic echoes—incantations—over jazz,
"doin the do," *c'est la vie*—
yeah, *la vie en rose*—
savouring a sudsy bath, frothy suds, a cream-soused coffee,
answering "Brown" to each nominal inquiry—
distanced from Regina's *Justice*-seekers—
a.k.a. "Furies"—eager to set the bloodhound posse bow-wow-wowing,
yapping, snarling, snapping.

(Me, unsuspecting—but *suspect*...
Now, just the despondent, foreign correspondent,
despicable—remiss—for preferring *Poetry*—overall—to *Silence.*)

*

Sick!

VERTIGO

XXVII.

I was distressed, and yes, distraught:
Underhanded, red-handed,
Steve'd mandated a hands-on *Obliteration*:
Ultra grisly facts, ultra perturbing.

He'd conducted a dry-ice *Incineration*.
(Ruddy smoke clumped like muddy run-off
slumped into dumped slabs of choked scarlet.)

Thus, I suffered *Vertigo* as inverting as *Vitiligo*.

*

Pondering Steve's evils, I roamed to Roma
to thunder, at John Cabot University—
versus bastards, dastards, adverse "retards"—
supreme in *Art*, yet defective in heart.
I didn't finger Steve; I damned Pound.
I slagged Caravaggio; I flagged Villon:

Smouldering was my sawdust ink—
the lines Dantean, burning cracks into paper—
while rain bleached white Rome's November-ashen cobblestones
and leached onto my black scalp.
I almost o.d.'d on sedatives
to salve my swollen, Byronic clubfoot—
(a brute infection bruited the sardonic comparison,
no fitting palliative to boot).

*

But my beckoning lecture effected, "Guilt by association,"
hectored reporters,
delving into every facet of their facetious selves,
to excrete twaddle, to squirt *Sensationalism* black as squid ink…
Hadn't I mollycoddled a murderer long-gone out his clink?

True: I'd hugged him in Cancún—
like a homey thug.
(Brown's mug? Butcher-wrapping-paper pink.)

XXVIII.

Wind-throttled leaves—gangrene-viral—
spiraled in Stuka-diving *Vertigo*; welled a Harpy din,
while I strove to rive from my mind a palooka—
all suave palaver,
a spook who gelled a mother into a cadaver...

*

A quarter-century after that cold-blood trial
of crackpot crackers—or rednecks imbecile—

a sallow gimp, I limped—
swallowing cephalexin and indomethacin
like shallow-in-the-glass, cocktail shrimp,
as I blimp-footed alongside Venice's *giallo*-unkempt canals—
pea-green, avocado-green, piss-green, lime-green,
olive-green, *Vinho-Verde*-green, seaweed green
(so hard to burn what's green)—
while *angina*-failure profs nailed up gallows:
But those are cataracts that were their eyes...

Thin, chapped lips chafed like scabbards. Tongues mimed swords.
Shrill nerves begat chilling *Invective*—
screwball skirmishes, defective blackboards,
ashtray tubs staggered with clubfoot-shaped stubs:
Could any pedagogue be honestly objective?

The *Worry*? Might I exculpate—exonerate—Steve,
plump up the Texas-size, big-ass bulk of his stanzas
let him bask—*in absentia*—in my cosseting applause?
(Well, the *Truth* is immaterial: It's what you believe.)

*

Steeled eyeglasses gaped blood-shot—bigoted.
Tongues hectic at each spigot'd wine-flask figured I'd elect S.K.—
and bury his victim in a grave forgot.

Best I be scolded black.
Scalded.

XXIX.

Unknowingly misinterpreted, I unknowingly misstep'd
(*faux-pas*'d), while dying sunflowers blackened (impossible
to butter up), each stalk—sooty, slackened. Implausible,
I crept, limped, puttered—gawking at Venice's canals—
a gimp, almost crying hourly from dour pain—
draining tubes of cephalexin and indomethacin—
banal as cocktail shrimp—
my rube's *Disability* dimpling a leg, a foot…

Witless yet was I that viper doctorates were hissing
(*angina* drivin em to ambush, camouflaged in dirt)—
my Regina lecture's purposing
was to defy George's kin and deify "Brown"—
so I'd cherish and nourish *Hurt*,
while flourishing mescal-slurred quotations
like some rascal chimp—
tasked to imp Brown's *Reputation* away from simple *Murder*.

(So, like Cinna the Poet, I should be pummelled down.)

Unawares, I watched leaves embark, cruise Venetian canals.
(Each wore eve's scotch-laved waves like House of Chanel's
autumn launches—ochre, cola, burnt-sienna, bronze, palls—
each *tranche*'d gondola borne to black, aquatic funerals…)
Next, I sat to dishes of minced black truffle,
vinegar-rinsed sardines, mustard-kerfuffled eggs,
wriggling spoils of jiggling oysters,
pear-and-cherries oiled by incensed brandy…

Innocent was I of academics, their *Panic* or *Fear*
plaquing each in a Woke, insomniac bed—
their worries (gone scurrilous in each querulous head)
soon mounting *La nouvelle trahison des clercs*…

Vertigo tumbled downward the mumblin Regina profs,
dumpin em out their slumpin Ivory—china-fragile—Tower.

XXX.

While I stumped under copper-green umbrella pines
beside copper-green canals
(ideal for jumpy suicides keening operatic finales),
then humped an ephemeral, pontoon bridge
to muse again on poems half-sunlight and half-sludge—
at Cimitero—San Michele—where moony, hero £* reclines;

way cross the gale-tossed Atlantic,
eggheads immoral as any dime-store Goebbels—
hullabaloo'd to bull's-eye "*that* black guy" as *Propaganda* fodder—
to sod-turn my grave as if unwrapping candy—
to bow-wow bawdy *Nonsense* and shoddy *Libel*—
such liminally criminal, triumphantly ghoulish crud...
To evince *Vertigo*...

*

So I stopped by £'s foot-traffic-rounded grave—
the sooty, engraved-graphic outcrop
of the now-grounded maestro
of each "Pisan Cantos" stave,
and mused how the poet had been impounded
for his doleful, wounding works.

Meanwhile, ruthlessly truthless clerks—
J.-Edgar-Hoover-murky, plotted a *Conjecture*—
hyperbolic, vitriolic, alcoholic, colic;
a scam was their thought, or, rather, shambolic:
To hector and bicker bout a lecture
unwritten, unresearched—a spectre!

---

* Salute Pound, Poundmaker—and "lb." Halfe (Pound-and-a-Half).

I'd nothing further to do in *Poetry*, but confess!

*

Meanwhile, a killer—gone south—stumbled his own path:
Sociopath.

SUSPICION

XXXI.

Sidling, foot-crippled, hobbling, funky, beside
those chunky, unbridled ripples stippling Venetian canals,
each pain-killing pill like shucked-shell shrimp—
I'd no hint that shrill, hacking, *insider* academics
were dishing (all fucked up), impish, about « a Golliwog
who might flog the wrong poet to the wrong room... »

So, despite any mollifying, fog-qualifying perfume
of dank cigarette smoke,
banking upwards like fluke Stukas—
each untoward palooka (each a joke)
figured to jail—nail—that "triggering" nigger, I,
pinch black me, inch by inch, winch me up for a lynching—
due to their hissed *Suspicion*
that I'd big up a poet
who'd done a blackguard *Crime*. So, brush-tarred I merited *Derision*.
(Imprisoned I was in lisping *Misprision*.)

*

Thus suddenly unspeakable became my lecture—
yet unwritten, let alone unspoken.
The *Ridiculous* had become *Sublime*!

So, that hectoring, conjecturing rednecks—
(some branded with protectorate doctorates)—
expectorated outta their Ivory Tower,
unduly, doubtlessly suspicious
that a foolhardy black minstrel-prof might
declaim a white poet, once a dastard—
but now presentably beaming like a sunflower—
no more a bastard, but as dreamy as sunlight...

XXXII.

While calico-coloured, oatmeal-discoloured, rain-frisked leaves
whisked Venetian canals with whiskey hues—
shades of drowned bees—
a rippling iridescence—a stippled palette—
each as dead as a tensely stubbed-out cigarette—

*

I didn't suspect all the *Suspicion*
being emitted, admitted, by danged scholars—
all their derisive, incisive, fangs and molars—
aimed at my jugular
(in vulgar *Ambition*)
to bleed out my dolichocephalic bighead,
i.e., my misbegotten, non-seraphic, too rotten egghead...

*

The Bible itself got chopped up as *Anathema*—
thanks to ass-phlegm blasphemies (*santorum*) shouted
during "Mergency meetins o da 'F/X'* Committee"
to hector—*heroically*—a lecture still a phantasmal schema...
Votes—grunted—shunted out each mouth's kitty.
Soon a stammering *Clamour* jackhammered my ears:
To help a poet, I'd exculpate a killer; forgive his arrears!
(Accusations never debated, so never doubted.)

*

* *Special Effects*: The funhouse-mirror side of *Ethics*?

98

Meanwhile, I was goblin-postured, hobbled in Venice—
oblivious to being sleazed by a cabal
(who smeared me as consanguineous with sanguine S.K.),
demarcating yours truly as a committed rat-fink—
due to audacious, salacious *Suspicion*—
and an Inquisitor's prognosticating diagnostics—
banal, bland, and so consummately *blanc*-and-*noir*—
it seemed almost as if our boudoirs were interchangeable…

XXXIII.

Venezia shed leaves while chill page leaves turned.
(The *News*? Each dread *Faith* wills its heretics burned.)

In Regina, now were gouts of snow—avalanches—
clouting every once-bare, provisionally virginal, black branch…

*

(Hear the pantomime of gasps as chalk rasped, smearing blackboards,
the yacking volume of an unerring hatchet job ratcheting up.

Snake-eyed commentators all dissertating *Suspicion*,
I'd exonerate a pervert and desecrate a poet…)

*

Thus, a degenerate *Intelligentsia*—
each teach silo'd in *Ignominy* and *Acrimony*—
fingered this *clerk* as a doctorated, decorated gremlin—
who'd alight from an Ivory Tower Kremlin—
linger—malinger—long enough—
to puff up Brown, huff at his persecutors.

But their misexecuted *Calumny*
excommunicated *Poesy,*
not *White Supremacy.*

*

So, I had to prove undiluted black—
according to slated drafts—
chalk as white as the fried tears
of sunlight-dried-up maggots…

XXXIV.

But to that tumultuous *Panic*, I was incognizant—
for moonlight chopped at my silhouette—
on my grape-splattered bib of earth—
with a slop of blush—*Rosato*—plus mythic giblets—
add-on splashes of white *vino* and a dash of anisette—
of wallet-shattering *Worth*—
at spiffy Locanda Montin Antico—
where iffy Pound had sought shelter from *Suspicion*.

*

Was not the right thing left for Pound to do only
to confess?
To figure the signature luminary
professing, blaring, his ineffaceable *Fascism*—
echoing a technique of *Candour*
(compatible with his truth—
tabulating how the swastika caught him—taut—
in its black, tarantula tentacles)?
Truly was this *koan* (公案) telegraphed—compassed—
by *The Pisan*—partisan—*Cantos* (nothin half-assed).
Meanwhile, I limped—a gimp—about that pirate marsh—
cuttlefish-ink-dark—
scuttling, outfitted with harsh cephalexin and indomethacin,
parked in my jaw, swallowed with phlegm.

*

(And Pound one more the poet exemplar—since Ovid—
since Lorca—since Mandelstam—since B.C. (Before COVID)—
since Malcolm X—since Aesop (th'Ethiope)—since Sappho—
since Juvenal—since Wilde—since Sade—since Cicero—
since Dante—since Moloise—since Riel—since Euripedes—

since Saro-Wiwa—since Brodsky—since Socrates—
since Yevtushenko—since Tsvetaeva—since Rushdie—
since Hikmet—since Pushkin—since Mapanje—
since Khashoggi—since Céline—since Ould al-Wahid—
since "Angela"—since Gramsci—since Eddy Said—
since Neruda—since Akhmatova—since Zola—to run afoul
of regime after regime of attempted regimen of the *Soul*.)

XXXV.

Already at Regina, on that *angina*-afflicted campus,
Wasn't I the blackboard, blacklisted catawampus?

Would I not natter bout a killer's limericks,
then buck-tooth guffaw—
a roly-poly Falstaff laugh—
as if a jolly Golliwog—
and call the throng to hardy-har-har along?

This prejudgement (*Prejudice*) spurred *Conniption*—
abrupt, corruptive seething—like that Roman mob
that blamed a blubbering poet*
for the knives forked slobbering into white-bread Caesar
till *le roi* torqued
bloody to the waist,
so the glamorous body appeared to be teething...

*

Abseiling over Venezia, and then availed of smoky Roma,
I was oblivious to insidious eves—
the *poesia*-induced comas—

pedants' bung-hole nostrils snotty with holier-than-thou *Suspicion*:

I'd puff up an ex-con poet—
buff him with academic kudos—
and take no guff from huffing censors—

---

* "In all ages and cultures, poets have been lost / before they could be found and encouraged."—Adrienne Rich (as quoted in Giovanna Riccio, *Vittorio* [2010]). So let us also salute *all* those Indigenous "whose voices have been lost too soon / and for all those whose voices are still singing" (Jesse Rae Archibald-Barber).

but tough out a family's still-raw *Grief*—
just slough it off, scoff…

Well, the *Truth* is immaterial—
like soil-drowned miners, bereft of official burial.

XXXVI.

So, with a foot palpably sore and implacably jittery—
and with indomethacin afoot and more cephalexin for eatery
(a placating, sedating *smörgåsbord*)—
I hobbled—bobbled—niggerish—egregious—wrong-headed—
among Venezia's *Vinho-Verde*-verdigris, leaded-green canals—
still asinine—yes—bout analphabetic,
F/X Committees—
ejaculating *Rhetoric*—briny—round and round—
circular as two crab-louses joined—
a gibberish fusing ragamuffin McCarthy
(Pinocchio Joe or dummy Charlie)
and a gewgaw "McGuffin"
(look it up).
Indeed, these anonymous, hyperventilating censors—
those smugly intransigent lugs—
as if shrunken heads (*tsantas*), smirking—
drunk on *Harrumph*, but *Bumf*-fed—
coined a pathetic *Suspicion*:
I'd quote a poet to okay his crime(s).

*

À Roma—not La Roma,
Distrito Federal (where Giovanna
and I'd tarried the Feb befo,
to testify—to *Poetry*—with then-believable Steve,
our bardic, "Hogtown" trio attuned to the *Bardo*—
avec guitars, keyboards, drums,
swooning with moonshine—
plums, almonds, oysters [a *smörgåsbord*]
at Las Muertas, i.e. *The Dead*)…

No, @ Roma (Italia), I roamed,
for John Cabot U. had headlined my talk—
"Must Poets Hang with Murderers?
A Meditation on Poetics and 'Justice.'"
I sought no *Sympathy* for devils—
Villon, Pound, Caravaggio, Burroughs, etc...
So I lounged in the gilt-and-marble lobby of Hotel Des Epoques,
oblivious to garbled but cockamamie *Gobbledygook*,
as I typed my typically lilting peroration,
elevating *Poetry*, not melting into *Silence*.

BLACKMAIL

XXXVII.

I took to transatlantic skies,
after brooking *Campari* without compare—
still unaware of the frantic Prairies'
inconsolable, indissoluble tears...

*

Well, I didn't know that P-h-Ds could carbon-copy McCarthy—
jeer on a cacophony of candid slanders and libels—
purvey a scheming *modus operandi*.
(*Violence* be the bonus—the brandy—of their Bibles!)

Perhaps the *F/X* Committee'd done voting
(while I sipped *Campari* so amply unawares,
there was *Panic* about what poets I'd be quoting)...
Slurs rocketed from mouths and pocketed in ears...

Unprofessional profs were acting like a church
flailing at *Heresy*, wherein bishops cheer on *Hearsay*—
satanically panicking (tongues, lungs, scarfing down fly larvae);
rhyming *Messiah* and *Mafia*, *black male* and *Blackmail*—
who couldn't concur that I should even research,
let alone speak to, how squatter *Justice* always fails...

Instead, maggots exited the butthole of each barfly,
barfing.

*

Lookit! To suggest that either *Poetry* (*Rhetoric*) or *Civil Rights*
must be *cancelled* to assert sincere *Solidarity*
with any community of righteous *Grievance*
is to posit a blatant *Tyranny*!

*

What else is left for me to do in *Poetry*,
but confess?

XXXVIII.

How else to vindicate violated Ms. George
if not to immolate my forged *corpus*—
so I go up in black smoke (doubtlessly)
in a corpse-disintegrating fire?

(Yet, what if gold basks bright in gloom—
like a muted sun?)

*

Thus, each tenured *saboteur* imagined
I'd devalue *Murder* as mere *marivaudage*,
that my quotations would stage a Kummerfield collage,
that my post-lecture signature would cha-cha-cha
over title pages, while I tittered, "Ha-ha-ha,"
embittering scandalous, post-prandial cocktails:
that I'd schmooze, outrageously, then snooze,
as if post-coital, not vital (unlike adroit black males)…

*

Thus, by callow, *giallo* journalists
(their facts firm as *Jello*)—
I got framed in a yellowed, *papier-mâché*-composed urinal—
while *ad hominem* ejaculations jizzed fizzy Op-Eds and blogs.

Such snazzy *Blackmail*.
One for the books!

XXXIX.

The assassination of my character
by a thousand paper cuts
by assassin-scribes (each a ham-fisted *saboteur*
clamouring to slam knives into a live 'Cinna the Poet')
is of no consequence, I profess.

The *News* established—oozed—such damnable,
undermining *Destabilization*!

*

Volatile goading, exploding vitriol, whirled up vile
tornadoes of acidic muck twirling outta bungholes.

Thus, soon, a headline billed G.E.C. as "the murderer"—
swilling the drastic noun—spilling blood on my name.
(*The Halifax Examiner*
thus also articulated my spectacular *Shame*.)

(Should I not sip unquenchable cyanide?

Yet, what shallow *Pity* fathoms reports of *Suicide*!)

*

Typeset lines proved elastic at typecasting—
promoting pure *Fuckery* as *Blackmail*—
to blacklist, blackball, blacken me
throughout the Caucasian-Supremacist North…

Did not pusillanimous campusites and apparatchiks
gang to sic unanimously scabrous reporters on me?

(Indeed, *Derision* could colour
any yellow journalist's
jaundiced *Rhetoric*.

. O! Beware that outright shit:
"Guilty by association!")

XL.

But Afro-Métis, Afro-Métif,
M'tis, Mestee, Mustee,
we be,
says Troy B. Bailey,
and also Negroes,
Mulattoes,
Africadians,
Melungeons
(burgundy our melanin),
Black Mi'kmaq,
Red Bones,
Brass Ankles,
Bois Brulés…

We Red/Black people
(who Communists & Anarchists adulate)
reno'd massas' homes,
wove poems of needlework,
groomed the stables,
coopered the barrels,
architected the ox-carts, the boats, the livery,
carriages, cabins, lofts,
and paddled and portaged canoes,
and translated Indigenous
to European
(see Mathieu da Costa)…

Yet, always was our genius
and our talent
subject to *Blackmail*…

So I was ID'd, not as *Literati*,
but as "niggerati," a "tribal wanna-be,"
a pettifoggin, Hogtown noggin—
agog, sayin he prefers,

over and above *Silence*,

Poesy.

SABOTEUR

XLI.

Testy came that "Banal" call, 23rd *décembre*, M.M.X.I.X.—
to pester—squalidly—whether I'd quote
a killer's verses (or anything he wrote)
in my lecture on *Femicide*—pandemic and obscene—
and yet so slippery to prosecute in Saskatchewan—
that *de facto* settler garrison…
(Too many *zwiebacks*, acquit of *Murder*, lounge, serene—
squatters acting squires:
Yep, sittin pretty with their pension cheques!)

A voice runny—tinny as tinnitus—afflicted my phone.
"*Guilt* by *Association*" was the select *koan** (人肉搜索).

I'd wished justly to examine *(In)Justice* through *Poetics*.

I testified, « A scholar's gotta research, gotta read,
to know what to write and report.
Can't pre-empt my unchalked talk. »

That response triggered a Catherine wheel of *Prejudice*—
much clapping and pissing, crapping and hissing.

*

Networking crocs—journos, clerks, docs—
suppurated briny weeping,
dribbling snot not unlike applesauce,

---

* The *rénròu sōusuo.*

121

swabbing their crabby, whining faces…
Each so truly make-up-false—
like a corpse faking its "sleeping."

(How they love to pig out on autopsies!
Drool over catalogues of homicides!)

*

Allen's website voyeured me—
la bête noire de la Tour d'ivoire—
in WANTED-poster style
(*nature-morte* in living *couleur*),
shoulder-to-shoulder with killer S.K.B.

But who was the real *saboteur*?

XLII.

Earth-breaking, sea-shaking, the lead "item" succeeded:
Walloped my quaking skull! (What *Nuance* was needed?)

« The poet refused to say whether he'd quote
the verse of a poet who slew a poet! »

Auscultating the *giallo*-plaintive radio, the *Purgolax* growls,
I heard howls gallop me like a runaway slave.
Those dog whistles upchucked outta gristle lungs—
brutal wind-tunnels, bristling exponential hoots,
snarky gargles, funky snarls, sordid chortles,
grisly monosyllables, Jezebel-style caterwauling,
amalgams of catcalls and brouhaha...

*

Otitis puffed—and tinnitus buffeted my ears:
My Warholian 15-Minutes of *Infamy*
welled outta th'Orwellian Two-Minutes *Hate*!
So, I had to be very publicly (if sneakily) whipped!

I was to be roasted in sulphur,
toasted—charred blacker—in flames,
while the savvy killer—*saboteur*—slouched in Mexico,
grouchy behind bottles of hooch.

How easy to knock over my *piñata* statue!
Unlike those dour white men in sour black robes—
empowered to discount *Rape* but count savage *Murder*
as just a case of frat boys gone wild.

*

Could I be shrunk down—hunkered in my basement—
a cave-dweller, like one of Plato's dupes,
stooped down in dirt, cooped up by *Hysteria*—
actually allergic to light?

XLIII.

« *Guilt by Association* » yapped the *Propaganda*—
the McCarthyite caca—
the Spanish Inquisition mantra—
the Kafka-inspired, ersatz *Pravda*!

Weaponized now were partisan hyenas
tee-heeing and hee-hawing—
unanimously braying out their unlocked kennels—
blithely baying after prey.

Nuttin's so tribal as da *diatribal*, eh?
(*Truth* bein immaterial.)

« Here's a poet who values *Poetry* more than *Silence*! »

Simpering yet judgemental, the yellow newsprint—
the striving, tongue-thumped, callow plosives,
the whimpering labials and clacking dentals—
did try to superimpose bloody'd white fingerprints
on my brown digits…
Cast me as a frame-up Cinna the Poet.

But weren't it two Boer-class, pallid "Native Sons"
who'd played each a catastrophic *saboteur*?

*

What else is left for me to do in *Poetry*,
but confess?

XLIV.

Shortly, Murph dialled up from YHZ to coax me
to flaunt my WANTED mug on *The National's*
#1 "ooze" story of Day 2 of 2020, vaunting
a ruse—a fiasco—a hoax.

Why?

I refused to play a conga-line "suspect," so Murph warned,
« If you don't appear, your lecture will get cancelled!
The [*Press*-ensured] *Pressure* will escalate! »

*

Uh-huh! Now, I understood
all the fundamentalist brouhaha
of my ballyhooed *Guilt* for *something*—
that all the ominous bellowing,
all the tut-tutting *Wrath*,
all the strutting *Outrage*
(sputum striding strident lips),
all the inestimable *Fracas*—
industrial grinding of molars,
banging of incisors,
barking of vigilante know-nothings
and digilante know-it-alls—
that all the banshee, bullhorn accusations
had to anatomize me as dug up, unearthed *Anathema*,
as being gleefully responsible for infinite bleeding—
an influx of skeletons—
unquantifiable skull fractures,
undeniable hemorrhages, stab wounds,
contusions, abrasions, bullet holes...

Guess who was the *saboteur*—
Public Enemy *Numero Uno*?!!

Meriting screams battering my eardrums,
plus clattering typewriter keys, tearing,
ripping, my gold onionskin…
To put the kibosh on my speech.

THE BIRDS

XLV.

Violently, but gaily, a tsunami of vitriol
my way whammed home! Trial-by-ordeal…
And weren't I no poet, just a callous gent,
a sham Métis—iniquitous, vile, arrogant?

Thus, a strutting aria gutted radios:
« He won't say what he will say
in a talk he *says* he hasn't yet written. »

(*Adios*! *Freedom of Thought, Conscience, Opinion,
Speech*: All quite *Verboten*!)

*

Soon, griping *Justice*-seekers joined the hunt-and-peck—
at beck-and-call
of cockamamie, Caucasoid dog whistles
hissing, promising blood to sweet the airwaves—
thus turning laptops into Lascaux cave walls—
folks whetting long knives round a comfy campfire
while chowing down on grey-brain-tissue and gristle.
The Birds—the buzzards, the hawks—
screeched, squawked, "He Should Have Known"!
What? That flour-power twins out the tweedy squatter-class
(so symptomatic of *Battery*, i.e., of crimson-splattered
clover and thistle, weeds and grass)
had lunged into and expunged a *mater*,
when, far from once-K.K.K.-enclave Saskatchewan,
I was a darky in K.K.K.-Konclave No'th Ca'lina,
where *explicit* Klansmen and Nazis—spiteful

(kops, complicit, standing by) "shot down in broad daylight"*
in Greensboro, *novembre*, M.C.M.L.X.X.X.—
albescent Communist and Afro-Christian confreres…
(*Requiescant in pace, mi dilecti, fortis, et specimen socii.*)

---

* Audit "The Ballot or the Bullet" by goodly Malcolm X.

XLVI.

I should have known?
Yeah, I'll say:
That some downpressed brethren and sistren seem ig'orant
that peckerwood Proud Boys rig up "Natives" as "niggers"…

(Check the O.P.P. at Ipperwash, ON, in M.C.M.X.C.V.—
i.e., the Kopper, *Criminally-Negligent* slaying of Dudley George
while their walky-talkies disgorged White-Is-Might *Jive*—
« We could bait ["the fucking Indians"—sneered the Premier]
 with a 2-4 of beer. »
« Yep, works down South—with watermelon! »
And the Canuck interlocutors—scheming Dixie-like executions—
giggled, chuckled, wriggled, buckled up, dreaming
of how to involve revolvers, rifles, and shotguns.)

I should've known that I'd appear an off-colour Métis—
an improv intellectual—
unapproved of and unimprovable…

I should have known that The Birds—vultures
(obscene rooks camouflaged as Kancel *Kulturalists**)—
would claw my preening books off library shelves,
would rip raw my quill-feathery attributes
down to the *disjecta membra* of *persona non grata*—
to cemetery my leathery, red-letter, black-and-white *corpus*…

---

* Engaged in a human-flesh hunt – the *rénròu sōusuo* (人肉搜索).

I should have known I'd be pursued
by birdbrains, quacks, grotty gulls, vultures, shitting,
plus pterodactyls, quick to blame-shame-frame
a dingy, black-singed poet—
to tar me with the squatters' gore.

Evermore.

XLVII.

As if I'd been imperious Leopold II crippling the Congolese—
swashbuckling bout and cashiering their appendages—
lopping a foot here, a hand there—
to fatten his coffers with diamonds and rubber trees—
Gregor Samsa*'s poetaster jaws squirted pus
to savage my visage. (His mouth a severe, gangrenous canker.)

Did he ache to undertake whimsical *Sabotage*?
To chop my *corpus* as if it could double for Khashoggi's?

Forgetful he seemed that yellow-bellied,
White—skin-dead—*Supremacism*
is as "native" (I pun)
as "starlight tours"
in Saskatchewan:

Ain't a civilian—not police—version
what befell Ms. George (to use reporters' metaphors)?

Anyway, what editor could repair his hack palaver,
his odes askew, his *sado*-spooky pages sagging,
gaping, like broken hinges, unsagacious?

(Lookit: A worse lyre—his—ain't never been strung;
But many a worse liar will get strung up...)

*

---

* This pseudonym refers to Kafka's Don-Marquis-"Archy"-like, insect protagonist.

Still, The Birds—like fulminating Furies—keep watch, survey,
set to pounce, to shit-bomb, shit-splatter—
to shit-plaster reputations;
so, soon heroic statuary be traumatized,
bespattered,
and besmirched is their oneiric *Daring*,
and scotched are their crowns
and their crotches blotched.

XLVIII.

The Birds—howling after carrion—tore at me
as if I were plump, puffed up roadkill
(already seeding, sowing, feeding, growing, bugs)—

as unabashedly "Guilty by association"

as if I were Cinna—
innocent of slabbing Caesar,
but stabbed dead anyway.

*

No matter: Beaked arrows,
piqued by my doctorate,
plus my preference for *Poetry*, not *Silence*,*
still narrowed the target

à moi.

And why not?
True poets' lungs and tongues ain't forgeries!

OMG & LOL…

*

* And yet, "The subject who is truly loyal to the Chief Magistrate will neither advise
nor submit to arbitrary measures."—Junius (*via* George Brown, 1844).

Okay: I was a simpleton—a paragon of *Insanity*—
to prefer *Poetry* to *Inarticulation*.

But did that fact justify
reporters' weaponization of *Opprobrium*—
to pervert *Opinion* to a pitch of *Calumny*?
So that *Suicide*—the plain idea—could chide my cranium?

Well, ain't black chaps everyone's fave scapegoats?

I should have known...

SABOTAGE

XLIX.

« Would Clarke be amiable to the killer—
or amenable to his *Talent*—
if he knew of the felon's damnable
Malice, his chilling, moral failure? »

That *hypothetical* set a lurid entourage
bobbling, squawking,
cabling and tabling and enabling *Sabotage*:

For wasn't I a hoity-toity, Hogtown prof—
persona non grata even in No Man's Land?

A defendant tried *in absentia*
by a kangaroo court jury
of the spuriously judgemental,
the vicariously indignant,
the fugitively spiteful—
tramps, scamps, scalawags, sleazebags—
all poised to pose as a posse,
so *Verity* could evaporate in *Persiflage*.

Sabotage!

(Those ball-peen hammers bashing through my skull—
splashing through my egghead skull...)

I tendered plural *mea culpa,*
bluesy arias;
I broadcast *apologia logopoeia apologia*—
Sorry sorry sorry sorry sorry—
for backing a *zwieback* cracker's
labyrinthine, four-sided, byzantine, four-square stanzas—
logging Mexico (more crapulent—& succulent—than Kansas)—

Sorry sorry sorry sorry sorry...

No more must I ever speak.

L.

I should have known—yep, *I should have known*—
that the crack *Outrage* of crackpots—
screeching like Bantustan *Mafiosi,*
would preach I'm best off necklaced with a car tire—
the rubber lit with unquenchable kerosene,
so that I, *la bête noire de la Tour d'ivoire*—
collared like Cinna the Poet—
could be tarred—torched—
while *mea culpa, mea culpa, mea culpa,* scorched my throat!

But was it I who aborted a mug's term mid the *Tantramarsh,*
so he could slug back pale marshmallows dotting hot chocolate
and ponder beat-up poets and thunder Beat poetry
(jazz-tinged, with beatific bongo-slapping)?
Was it I who got S.K.
a *Get-Outta-Jail-Early* passport
and a pseudonym,
to let him skip—smug—to Mexico?

*

But epically malignant, their mouths niggling o'er *errata*—
robed-n-tassell'd skunks topping the hierarchy of the crapper—
those hellacious cannibals posing—dapper—as dentists—
who rinse their chaps with piss
(and who like to swizzle it—sizzling),
craved my pigmentation engraved with scarlet stigmata...

Via Sabotage!

LI.

S.K.'s catastrophic *Transgression*
justified a Gothic *fatwa*
of *pur et dur Suppression*?

To: "*maintiens le droit*"?

Lookit! That's the facile appeal to appalling populists—
their crabby shadows, their shabby credos

(the *National Enquirer* readership—
all those who've reached the end of *Democracy*—
and their Donald John Trump leadership,
happy to bully-pulpit *Mobocracy*)...

Well, those types are—sayeth Mao—
"Left in form but Right (*Fascist*) in essence."
The passionate fusillades of their lungs?
The pure pitch of *Rage*, sullying any *Sense*...

*

Some journalists—
all—ahem—"guilty by association"—
fabricated *Sabotage*—

retailing the rigid letters of *Stereotype*—
hailing the tarred *Poesy* of jaundiced newsprint...

To exasperate *Reason* and exculpate *Reaction*;
to encourage *Revulsion* and exacerbate *Regression*!

LII.

Yes, I'd granted Samaritan *Succour*
to a conniving killer
(who carried himself as if he'd only ever been a cherub
never a butcher)…
So, was I the printer's devil to his Beelzebub?

Apoplectic, *headhunters* were all halitosis at one end
and diarrhea at the other—
but intersectioned were their ends,
their bottom-lines:

Because it was a *Damnation* that Kummerfield-Brown
could morph from ex-con
into a bard omniscient of Ginsberg
and reminiscent of Ferlinghetti,
and then task Giovanna and I
to rusticate in May-he-co, uncask tequila and rye—
and recite to Tijuana jazz and marijuana—
verses from our triad's (myriad-lyric'd) chapbook,
Two Hogtown Poets / Psicogeografia
(Libros del Marqués,
Ciudad de México,
M.M.X.I.X.),
when we were inspired and relaxed and the air was silk—

and two poets didn't know about THE *Sabotage*:
That a third poet (our host)
had disappeared—muted—a fourth, Ms. George,
Nature's poet, undying ghost.

*

But what was *my Guilt*?

Oy!

Is there anything else for me to do in *Poetry*,
but confess?

I CONFESS

LIII.

2 days after becoming
"A sixty-year-old smiling public man" (Yeats);
2 days after *confit de canard et calvados*
(and toasts from Giovanna—
the liquid manna of *amore*),
and a 100% silk tie milking a 10th-century Persian design—
boasting "the dynamism of pluralism"—
gift-boxed by the Aga Khan Museum…

*

I glided—YYZ to YHZ—
to tipple handcrafted bitters
in the heart of downtown hometown;
to orate *Poesy* to my homeys—
folks who've always had my back.

(And my African Baptist Saviour be
Who He Is:
Not even roofing nails could seal the lid
on X's coffin!)

*

And I recollected here's where Black sistah & *proxenetist*
(just like Pamela George)—
Catherine Wright, only 26, in 1985,
got stabbed to death—
that March 8th—
11 times stabbed—
by whiteface Patrick Slaney
who got but 7 years
(a wrist-slap sorta sentence)
and served but 3 for his *Womanslaughter*...

*

Aye, Nova SKKKotia doth resemble—
pointedly—
SasKKKatchewan sometime...

I confess!

LIV.

In Halifax, the plaintive Atlantic
hurled *Grief* against snow-fringed boulders
at Black Rock Beach—
to blackly wash away the white encrustations;
each black-ink glare akin to flickering razors.

I confess I watched waves splinter, scintillate...

*

Suddenly, I recalled Ms. Catherine Wright:*
Black woman, sistah, Africadian, Afro-Baptist—
who got stabbed 11 times,
11 times,
stabbed 11 times—
by a gent of Euro descent, Mr. Patrick Slaney—
well-groomed in court—
who'd gone whole-hog on Ms. Wright—
mater et proxenetist—
stabbed her 11 times—
left her dying bleeding body
to freeze in a Haligonian gutter
amid garbage, mouldered snow, black ice—
March 8, 1985—
and how Mr. Slaney served
just 3 years for *Womanslaughter...*

---

* "The offence was a particularly brutal stabbing and the victim died from deplorable acts of extreme and excessive violence." (R. v. Slaney, Nova Scotia Supreme Court, Appeal Division. Oral judgement: September 18, 1986.)

Throughout Africadia, arias of *Anguish*
wracked our "Indigenous Black"
reserves—Bantustans—townships:
Ululating *Red—Black—Green*.

*

All while the Atlantic wiped
white rime off black boulders
on the Haligonian beachhead.

LV.

While black waters scoured snow-topped boulders—
and the snow-twisted, grating wind turned black
in the draconian, unstoppable waves,
my *Memory* caved—toppled back—35 years…

Cue "The Ballad of Catherine Wright"*:

« You walk Halifax streets that white men walk,
Hear their gabble condemn the way you talk.
They shut their doors and called you dumb.
They wouldn't hire you, only sell you junk.

« You ask for *Justice*, but nothing's right.
Day work ain't here, so you take the night…
Then, Patrick Slaney sprang a cantankerous knife…

« You didn't have time to parry his hands:
His blade slashed—dashed—your precarious plans!
Your blood crashed into a filthy, snowy gutter;
It washed into a strange *étang*…

« Jurors thought ya deserved to die, God's daughter:
Slaney stabbed 11 times but only got *Manslaughter*.

« This blood-stained "Justice" would set Judas free,
Stab down Mary, lynch Jesus from a tree…
We woke the morning of your dark death:
Found South Africa right on our doorsteps… »

---

* "[T]he death of [Catherine Wright] resulted from violent, vicious and brutal stab-bing…" (R. v. Slaney, Nova Scotia Supreme Court, Appeal Division. Oral judgement: September 18, 1986.)

Well, our bread is *pain* and our blood is *sang*.

(An Afro-Métis poet, I wield *Witness*!)

I confess!

LVI.

I heard of vulgar machinations—
unaccountable clerks—unreal pedants—
quite countless at the University of Regina,
calling unabashedly for *Silencing.*[*]

Never unseasonably bookish,
these hacks (cackling like jackals)—
assholes in the public domain—
staged Academia as a Gulag...

*

So, on that heart-felt Valentine's Day,
I lifted midnight Scotch flights with a militant sect
of New Scottish and/or *Black Watch* Scotians:

I confess we did *not* confuse
human *nature* with juridical *culture*
(white faces, black robes),

but did *scruple* to *couple*
settlers' genocidal *minds* to their whelps' homicidal *hands*...

*

Then: *Eight Miles High* time to accompany *la bellissima*—

---

[*] Often folks try "to immunize from criticism" their dearest opinions. How? By "stigmatizing those who dissent ... or by demanding that they be excluded from campuses..." (Robert George & Cornel West). See Harry C. Boyte, *Academic Matters* (Spring 2017), p. 29.

amorissima Giovanna—
to Cuba (Caya Coco)—
rococo with solar solace and volcanic rum…
To blend French *brut*—redolent of pears—with Finnish vodka…

(Try *that* to negate the fate of Cinna the Poet—
beseeching the Roman mob,
busy clobbering him down; his blood squabbling?)

LVII.

McGill's Wendell Nii Laryea Adjetey determined:
"The misinformation campaign and online hysteria
made Clarke a *cause célèbre*.
Some journalists placated the mob,
portraying him as guilty.
Since when did polling social media—
the woke regime's judge and jury—
become the new mode of journalism?"

Furthermore, Adjetey attested, in his Op-Ed,
the whole "Regina Fiasco" was
a "non-sensational story."

So what drove all the *Calumny*,
all the kvetching and hiss of *Hypocrisy*,
all the wretched crud, all that sloshed piss?

Racism surfacing—prefacing—*Fascism*?[*]

*

Calgary Herald columnist Catherine Ford's analysis[**]
(only a "3-minute read" counsels the website):
"Clarke himself did nothing wrong"
in editing S.K.'s poetry…
"[B]ut in cancel culture
["This mob-bullying tactic"]

[*] See *The Toronto Star*, January 21, 2020.
[**] January 8, 2020.

161

the mere notion he had aided …
a killer …
of a First Nations' woman,
became the lightning rod for anger."

Yes, antique *Anger* resuscitated
due to an atrocious *Crime*—
never truly expiated
(just like every other time).

*

I confess:
Absurdities foster atrocities (Voltaire).

& *Ferment* fosters torments…

*

Time to revive the Party Rhinoceros—
those truly bogus politicos—
i.e., wise-guy clowns who expose
courts all kangaroos, parliaments all Pinocchios.

LVIII.

My pro-Indigenous arguments (published)
and Afro-Métis status
got whited out, blacklisted, red-lined…

One-sided as unenlightened thunder
clamoured the frenzy of *Denigration*—
stammered the ethnic-cleansing *Defamation*.
Blunder upon blunder upon blunder!

Soon, airwaves clogged with dogmatic monologues
dogging me, so eager to flog *ye olde* scapegoat Golliwog.

*

Still, a poet has to trust in *Poetry*,
not *Silence*, not *Silencing*,
not ephemeral testimonials.
I conjured Malcolm X, first silenced
by the Nation of Islam's *fatwa*
and then by its roaring shotguns.
But X's voice soar louder than ever—
imploring—explosive—like Cuban surf!
(*Truth* be never immaterial!)

*

So, witness S.K.'s excretions,
his feces-eating grin, greasy sourness,
gangrenous ghoulishness,
back a drawn-and-quartered-century of Aprils—
while angels were indifferent
to two psychos enacting bloodthirsty *Frenzy*,
their frank fists like four pistons—
who knew that the Boer *(In)Justice* system would blame
an Indigenous woman for her own (*Rape* and) *Murder*—
and treat her killers as if they were juveniles who'd jaywalked—
and treat her killers as if they were juveniles who'd jaywalked…

I confess!

FRENZY

LIX.

Frenzy diabolical! Furies aping apostolic breath!
To quote a murderer's poetry was
to abet a mother's being punched to death.

Hectored Allen, December 23rd, M.M.X.I.X.,
by phone, « Pray tell what poets you might cite,
pre-empt your lecture *before* you even write.

« Disclose *à moi* thy evidence, Doc Clarke,
thy proof that squatter-class Saskatchewanian poets
get away with *Murder* [*She Wrote*] by rote.

« I beg thee: Go on the record, go on the record:
An alarming scenario has all Regina panic-stricken—
that thou might quote a killer's lyrics in thy lecture.

« There's *Trauma*—histrionic—o'er thy scheduled talk.
There's *Upset*—apocalyptic—plus emotional *Shock*.
The tensions are *pandemic* » [my word, but it seems right].

Surprised by her tale of startling *Crisis*, I advised—
pointedly—*Allen*, "Everybody should just relax."
[I.e., I haven't writ a word, haven't researched facts.]

Naturally, the grotty, trophy clip portrayed
this *dupe* as haughty. The endless looping of the select
white noise—no context to be detected—betrayed

a callous caricature. *Incroyable—soudainement,*
j'étais une bête noire dans la Tour d'ivoire—
an unscrupulous *niggard* and duplicitous *à croire.*

But all I'd said—all filters and blinders off—was,
« I will take the time to read and analyze,
then produce conclusions. » Just what a scholar does!

(But with bunk, bluster, and bullshit, cancerous hustlers—
affianced to a gussied-up McCarthyism—
advanced, in their cussed *praxis,* the up-thrust axe of *Fascism.*)

---

* An illiterate euphemism.

LX.

To realize a *giallo*-eyes-wide-shut *effect*,
yellow, bellowing journalists confected *Affect*.

(See *Knowledge, Power, and Academic Freedom,*
by Joan Wallach Scott, reviewed by Robin Whitaker,
in *bulletin*, 67.1, December-January 2020,

wherein Whitaker quotes Scott's worry
"'Incivility' may be 'the new McCarthyism.'"
And "Incivility targets affect," p. 9.)*

So, I got blacked out and blackballed.
And my *Social Justice* writings benighted!
And my *Identity* blighted out!

But few acted appalled…

*

The *Frenzy?*
Woozy *Vilification* and bluesy *Victimization*.

I was the shade of Shakespeare's Cinna the Poet—
if not blamed doubtfully for *Murder*, or murdered *sans* a doubt.

*

---

* Thus, on January 23, 2020, in the *Regina Leader-Post*, Chasity Delorme declared,
« Truth and Reconciliation, the movement, needs to supersede freedom of academic
speech. » Yet, without *Academic Freedom* (to research, to inquire, to exchange ideas,
to question, to teach, to challenge), I say, *Freedom* becomes merely "academic."

True: At least I still breathed!
I'd not been turfed up, shovelled over.
I was not debilitated lilies flung down on a casket.
I was (not yet) only fountain-pen ink shivering a sheet.

LXI.

The *Frenzy* staged a *Bedlam* carnival, a "Bill Lynch" freak-show!
Why? Because the sequence of consequences—
permitting defendants their postures and pretenses—
had seemed calculated to let two clear killers go.

Yet, the Furies skirted the Caucasian courts; so, the *Frenzy*
clawed for me, as if I were the callow outlaw, the sallow killer;
then, dirty journalists saw my c.v. ethnically cleansed;
and my poems got dumped and my novels went to swill.

*

While charivari and brouhaha circus'd through broadband,
S.K. typed a drunk note, "Ho! Ho! Ho! Now you know
what it feels like!" As if I deserved his merited brand
and *Degradation*! Next, he emailed, *avec* much psycho
Gumption, "I'll never say I'm sorry." *Touché*: No "Truth
and Reconciliation"—blarney and bromides—for him!
He told a sister poet: "I didn't murder anyone." [Gulp of vermouth.]
"Neither did Alex. We committed manslaughter." [Ahem.]
"Still most civilized countries understand the difference.
If you have chosen to think otherwise, I think that would be too bad."
Yessum, the shameful sociopath got no defence.

*

But, nor do rabid gangstalkers, that rabble, each mouth gabbling mad...

(Yep! Rather than obliterate *Injustice* and *Racism*, "advocates"
bayed like banshees to beg a killer's corpus be stabbed to bits!)

*

Thus transpired a comedy of *Malice*
inspired by a black-comic *canard*:
To study *Poetry* is to authorize *Crime*.

LXII.

Frenzy:

- Heather Mallick, in her *Toronto Star* column (January 7, 2020), slagged me as a "general honours magnet," and then sneered, "If that's true [that I didn't know about S.K.'s crime until September 2019], he had fourteen years to ask." An *ad hominem* attack got chased by an asinine assertion.

- A *Halifax Examiner* critique (January 12, 2020) floated a reckless headline: "George Elliott Clarke, the murderer, and the murdered woman." It slanders itself.

- The University of King's College (Halifax) withdrew—lickety-split—my January 10, 2020, invitation to address their Creative Non-Fiction students in Toronto.

- Toronto's Indigenous radio station, ELMNT-FM, invited me on-air on January 13, 2020, to discuss my "side of things," then pulled the interview from its website two days later. The reason? I was "too one-sided."

- A poet who'd begged me in Fall 2019 for a blurb for his forthcoming volume wrote to say that the publisher had decided to strip it from the cover.

- Fearing that it could trigger "misunderstanding," a poet's editor wrote to bade me omit the term *gynecology* that I'd used to intro her collected poetry. Done. My intro still got spiked.

- An esteemed Hogtown literary press squashed a Black History Month event intended to honour my mentoring of its African-Canadian author.

• The Federation of Sovereign Indigenous Nations, the Assembly of Manitoba Chiefs, the First Nations University Student Association, and Idle No More: Each pronounced its denouncing *fatwa*.

• A Haligonian celebration of my poetry was scuttled due to concern that a bank could reconsider its Black History Month funding if my name darkened the program.

• Anonymous emails counselled, "Go Fuck Yourself" and/or "Drop Dead." *Et cetera.*

Frenzy!

(What *Journalism* as yellow as a urinal crystallizes:
Public *Opinion* gangrened to *Hatred*—

the axe-grind of the dime-store Goebbels—

Truth be immaterial.)

LXIII.

Frenzy:

February 4, 2020

Dear Professor:

We are writing to convey our concerns about plans to feature George Elliott Clarke as a guest speaker at the 2020 Congress of the Humanities and Social Sciences (Congress). In light of the recent controversy surrounding Mr. Clarke, we are urging the Canadian Comparative Literature Association (CCLA) to reconsider a programming decision that we fear will be perceived as insensitive and disrespectful to Indigenous communities.

Our conversations with Federation members over the past few days, including the President of the Indigenous Literary Studies Association (ILSA), have led us to conclude that hosting this event will re-ignite a divisive public controversy that will go against the purpose and spirit of Congress, and distract media, members of the public and Congress attendees from other essential conversations.

As Congress organizers, we support free expression and the exchange of ideas, as well as open, critically engaged and sometimes challenging discourse. However, as University of Regina President and Vice-Chancellor Dr. Vianne Timmons stated recently, if speech "serves to cause hurt [...], we have to consider it carefully."* In this particular context, we firmly

---

* Yet, Dr. Timmons telephoned me at my home to express her concerns for my well-being and her fears about a scheduled demonstration at the U. of R. on January 23, 2020.

believe that inviting George Elliott Clarke to speak at Congress could make many attendees feel unwelcome or even unsafe, especially Indigenous scholars and graduate students.

This is not a matter of silencing Mr. Clarke, but rather a matter of assessing judiciously the choice of keynote speakers we host, in light of the message that choice sends to communities and the public. In this respect, we are requesting that the CCLA reconsider its decision to maintain George Elliott Clarke in its Congress program.

Thank you for your consideration. We are available to discuss this matter with you at any time, and to work together to make Congress 2020 a great success for all involved.

LXIV.

Frenzy![*]

11 February 2020

Dear Professor George Elliot [sic] Clarke,

We have received a number of requests to reconsider our invitation for you to keynote our conference on June 1, 2020. Our partner association withdrew their support following a lengthy debate among their Executive. The Federation of Humanities and Social Sciences also expressed concern regarding our plans. Although both parties underlined our autonomy in choosing keynote speakers, the CCLA Executive had to weigh the sensitive nature of the concerns that were expressed. We have made a difficult majority decision to seek an alternative speaker for this event. We don't hold anyone personally accountable for this outcome. What we have all agreed on is that plans for this keynote event have been divisive, and that perpetuating these divisions will ultimately prove to be a distraction – if not for Congress as a whole, certainly for us. Again, CCLA does not make any judgements about the circumstances that have led to this outcome. We do, however, recognize that some who are closer to the issues than we are feel very strongly, and we hope the matter is resolved in an appropriate space for discussion and healing.

[*] I have framed this letter and it hangs in my University of Toronto office.

LXV.

My Esteemed Academic Colleagues of the CCLA/ACLC:

I respect the courage that you exercised in revoking the invitation to me to address yourselves at Congress 2020 at Western University on June 1, 2020. Surely, it was difficult to choose between satisfying the "number of requests" that you received to "reconsider our invitation" and trying to honour liberal notions of due process (such as collecting evidence, even testimony, maybe even from "the accused"), let alone abiding such tricky Charter rights as *Freedom of Expression* and *Freedom of Association*, or even practices of dialogue and debate, although these irksome verbs often can lead to "bridging divides" (which is, I note with due astonishment, the theme of Congress 2020).

In recognition of the bravery that you have demonstrated, I beg you to mail to me a new copy of your February 11, 2020, missive, on your official CCLA / ACLC letterhead, with not a single change in diction or punctuation (though you could spell "Elliott" attentively). I do task you to sign your names—each of you, in indelible ink—beside its appearance in the typed list. I pray that you will look kindly upon my request and act with just pride to present me with signatures that will illuminate your individual expressions of academic heroism. Please do not let undue *Modesty* prevent you from registering, in each distinctive hand, your valiant upholding of silencing, shunning, and censorship.

Yours very truly,

GEORGE ELLIOTT CLARKE*

P.S. Did *Frenzy* gobsmack yas?
Was yas all innocent of *Thought*?

---

* Cinna the Poet.

LXVI.

The *cancellaires*—the *digilantes*—
luxuriate in one *Truth*:[*]

Few institutions purposed to buttress
Freedom of Expression will, in fact, do so,
for it is *always* messy politics:
Either the speech is unpopular or the speaker is;
or the cause is murky and the opposition stark;
or the CROWD is empowered and LOUD,
the dissenters marginalized and dissed.

Thus, soon materialized that letter, on February 11, 2020,
signed by 13 academics[**]—
revoking my invite to speak at their *scholarly* gathering,
due to unspecified allegations
I was never permitted to address.
Rather, they verified my *Ignominy.*

[*] They do rue one fact: Their "gangsta" action—anonymous and cowardly—can destroy vulnerable *individuals* (whatever ephemeral "justice" that brings), but they are resolutely impotent *versus* truly oppressive *institutions.*

[**] For the record, they constituted the Executive of the Canadian Comparative Literature Association and were signatories to a one-sided, pro-silencing missive of February 11, 2020:
Joshua Synenko, President
Doris Hambuch, Vice President
Jerry White, Treasurer
Mark Terry, Media and Communications Officer
Laurence Sylvain, Early Career Scholar Representative
Albert Braz, Member at Large
Lee Dylan Campbell, Member at Large
Schlomo Gleibman, Member at Large
Jack Hang-tat Leong, Member at Large
Jessica Tsui-yan Li, Past President
Irene Sywenky, Editor, *Canadian Review of Comparative Literature*
Susan Ingram, WebSys Admin
Jeanne Matthieu-Lessard, Translator

Whatever the merits of that status—
13 *clercs*—
persons imagined to favour facts—
afforded me no hearing, no testimony,
yet voted for my banning.
Plea and appeal disallowed.

Freedom of Speech & *Opinion* & *Conscience*?
All nixed as if unconstitutional folderol!

Well, that's what happens when (effete) aesthetes—
or journalists—
pitch out *Inquiry*

to pitch *Inquisition*…

Frenzy!

LXVII.

March 9, 2020

Dear Professor:

We are writing further to our letter of February 4, 2020, regarding a Congress event featuring Professor George Elliott Clarke.

We wrote our letter to help inform your internal deliberations about the event. However, as we have subsequently realized, the information we provided was incomplete. In our determination to convey concerns of ours and other Congress participants, we did not fully appreciate the possible implications on freedom of expression.

We are committed to freedom of expression and recognize that it is a fundamental principle on campus and essential to the pursuit of truth, the advancement of learning and the dissemination of knowledge. While there are limits to freedom of expression, such as hate speech, incitement to violence, and threats to physical safety, we have no reason to believe that these are applicable to Professor Clarke's lecture.

In closing, we can confirm that Professor Clarke will be speaking at Congress on June 1, 2020, at an event organized by the Association of Italian Canadian Writers (AICW).

*

[And the AICW is Botticellian cellos
and cellared *Folonari*

(Pinot Grigio di Venezia)—
and the answer to *Frenzy*
be *Poesia*.

I laud Joe *e* Gio:[*]
Courage's echo.]

[*] Pivato / Riccio.

LXVIII.

Steady Frenzy!

<u>Zoom Security Report</u>

The date, time and time-zone this took place, October 3, 2020, Pacific time 11:45 A.M. -1:45 p.m.

4. the participant name(s) of the intruder(s), see below

5. a description of what occurred during the meeting and how the intruders violated Zoom's terms of service.
k. sailor (D. Sailor)
Omu_Negru69@_____

He unmuted himself and made a very disturbing racist comment on one of our guest speakers who is black. He said, "Madame, would you get that nigger George Elliott Clarke off your screen?"*

---

* This Zoom Report is factual. However, I have altered the email address and changed the name of the sender, not because the miscreant deserves to have his privacy preserved, but because I cannot prove that he was the person who made the statement. But there are witnesses to his trespass, including my fine comrade-poets, Alice Major, Al Moritz, and Anna Yin. In addition, it is useful to note that "*omu negru*" is Romanian for "black man," a handle that is presumably ironic. Finally, while I could have expected *Criticism* over my once-camaraderie with an ex-con poet, I had not suspected *Racism* as an underlying catalyst—until snow-white venom came volleying at me eyes-n-ears.

BACKWORDS

LXIX.

Impasto be my bumpy *Strategy*, my gusto *Poetic*:

To squirt or heap lightning!
To clump or melt thunder!

To protest probable thousands of unmarked graves
of Indigenous and Métis children,
incarcerated in government-sanctioned, church-run schools…

How else to have *Truth* (*History* fully recovered)
and *Reconciliation* (*Reparations* for inhuman crimes)?

Down with the paralysis of *Grief*!
Down with the stasis of *Apology*!

Overthrow the myth of *White Supremacy*
and the *Settler Superiority Complex*
that continues to make the seizures of children,
the wrongful jailing and injury of children,
the miseducation of children,
and even their lonesome deaths and loathsome burials,
a predictable outcome of their governors' indictable offenses.

Demolish the hierarchy of ethnicities that pits European Caucasians
against Black/Indigenous/People of Colour;
that ranks settler institutions above Indigenous cultures,
that situates Indigenous and Black people at the bottom,
silenced in prisons, suffering in poverty,
or, worse, our children disappeared and our graves desecrated.

*

Yet, *never* will I agree that *Poetry* (*Rhetoric*) or *Civil Rights*
must be *cancelled* to prove *Solidarity*
with any community of righteous *Grievance,*
lest I submit to positive, blatant *Tyranny.*

LXX.

There's nothing left for me to do in *Poetry*,
save to council, yep, "I confess":
I've witnessed my notorious *Elsehood*!
(My Afro-Métis visage—
that unimaginable coffee-colour—
appears treasonable, mortuary-ready,
no shadow of a doubt!)

Too, the rickety squiggles my pen scrawls so poorly
can never be wholeheartily unsullied…
(Every line's a type of *Blackmail?*)

*

Remember Ms. George:
Her wine-dark eyes, her pine-dark hair,
the sable glint of her ink, unsullied,
until radio'd blues stained the night

when two psychos defined her Cree spirit as *expendable*;
and those unfeeling saboteurs—
geniuses of *Obliteration*—
attacked a matrix of verse,
annulling a mother as if smashing a fly;
where Treaty 4 was lemon-inked
(the guarantees seeming *Etch-A-Sketch* wonky—
too prone to quaking *Erasure* and/or *Sabotage*)…

*

(In a fugue-state—a *Frenzy*—
The Birds swooping in *Vertigo*—
taking *Suspicion* as their guide—
dive-bomb local-and-foreign correspondent.)

*

But I's a poet who values *Poetry* more than *Silence*...

*

This paper curls as it burns,
and the black ink flickers, smudged,
fluting skyward as smoke.

Dear Reader:

Beauty *must be tortured first*
before it confesses to a golden ratio…
  —Luciano Iacobelli, *Dolor Midnight*

The Alfred Hitchcock film titles are not imaginary. (The *Truth* is immaterial.)

This essay-in-poetry was occasioned by True (*Crime*) events perpetrated a quarter-century ago that yet reverberate – to the extent that I was persecuted in early 2020 for my refusal to rehearse in public an *unwritten* essay sampling Saskatchewan poets for their perspectives on anti-Indigenous violence. Worse, I was allotted no way to rebut scurrilous attacks. This poem is my answer.

My once-friendship with poet Stephen Tyler Kummerfield-Brown – *suspended* when he confessed his 1995 *Crime* to me in September 2019 – *ended* in January 2020 when he refused to express public *Remorse* for his role in the slaying of Pamela Jean George. When and where was I dishonourable?

Yes, Kummerfield-Brown benefitted from a grotesquely lenient *Justice* system, and then *Magic* that eased his way – a convicted killer – into and out of a Club Fed prison and then into a new life – with a new surname – in Mexico. Still, the remedy for squatter *(In)Justice* is not to silence others, but to *Indigenize* the justice system, starting with the Supreme Court of Canada.

While cowards caved before the Kancel *Kultur* Kampaign to "blacken" me, other bodies proved righteous: The Aga Khan Museum, the Association of Italian-Canadian Writers, the Delmore "Buddy" Daye Learning Institute, The Ontario Poetry Society, *The Trinity Review*, the University of Toronto, and Victoria University. (But *silent* remained the League of Canadian Poets and the Writers' Union of Canada.) Several individuals also tendered *Nurture*. They should know that I love them for their courage, their respectable upholding of *Truth*, and their rejection of Orwellian tactics – <u>*even when*</u> such get broached as plaints vs. *Injustice*.

I thank H. Archibald Kaiser, Professor, Schulich School of Law and Department of Psychiatry, Faculty of Medicine, Dalhousie University, for leading me to documents dissecting the 1985 homicide upon Ms. Catherine Wright. Dr. Sonia Labatt, Ph.D., and Victoria University (*via* The E.J. Pratt Professorship at the University of Toronto), yielded sustenance that permitted me to author this poem on Manitoulin Island (ON), at Colchester (ON), and in Toronto (ON).

I thank Barry Callaghan and Michael Callaghan for publishing this book – my third volume alongside the hundreds by an incredible commune of "Exiles"… They are heroic, compassionate, and wise. They also gave me counsel that I have essayed to reflect.

I confess that my bracingly critical readers and editors – Marsha Boulton, Barry Callaghan, Michael Callaghan, Nina Callaghan, Marco Katz Montiel, Giovanna Riccio, Janet Somerville, and Paul Zemokhol – are the sources of all *Beauty* herein. Any wrongs redound on me alone.

And for what is it that all good people have bled?
Beauty / Liberty / Equality / Dignity.

GEORGE ELLIOTT CLARKE

The 4th Poet Laureate of Toronto (2012-15) and the 7th Parliamentary/ Canadian Poet Laureate (2016-17), George Elliott Clarke is a revered artist in song, drama, fiction, screenplay, essays, and poetry.

His publications number titles in Braille, Chinese, Italian, and Romanian.

Born in Windsor, Nova Scotia, in 1960, Clarke is a matrilineal descendant of African-Americans and Cherokee (peoples transported to Nova Scotia during the War of 1812) and a patrilineal descendant of an African-American great-grandfather and a Jamaican grandfather. He be Afro-Métis.

Educated at the University of Waterloo, Dalhousie University, and Queen's University, Clarke is a pioneering scholar of African-Canadian literature. The inaugural E. J. Pratt Professor of Canadian Literature at the University of Toronto, Clarke has taught at Duke, McGill, the University of British Columbia, and Harvard.

He holds eight honorary doctorates, plus appointments to the Order of Nova Scotia and the Order of Canada at the rank of Officer. Also he is a Fellow of the Royal Canadian Geographical Society.

His recognitions include the Bellagio Center Fellowship, the Pierre Elliott Trudeau Fellows Prize, the Governor-General's Award for Poetry, the National Magazine Gold Award for Poetry, the Premiul Poesis (Romania), the Dartmouth Book Award for Fiction, the Eric Hoffer Book Award for Poetry (US), International Fellow Poet—Encyclopedic Poetry School Trophy (China), and the Dr. Martin Luther King Jr. Achievement Award. In 2021, he was named a Life Member of the League of Canadian Poets.

Byron / Shelley / Keats / & a Misfit, Roma, Italia, 2018. Photograph by Giovanna Riccio.

Clarke's work is the subject of *Africadian Atlantic: Essays on George Elliott Clarke* (2012), edited by Joseph Pivato, as well as a substantial entry in *Contemporary Literary Criticism*, volume 459 (2020), also overseen by Professor Pivato.